DURHAM COMPANY

DURHAM COMPANY

*

UNA POPE-HENNESSY

1941

CHATTO & WINDUS

LONDON

PUBLISHED BY

Chatto & Windus

LONDON

★

The Macmillan Company
of Canada, Limited

TORONTO

CONTENTS

*

*

TO RICHARD

ILLUSTRATIONS

*

*

INTRODUCTION

INTRODUCTION

At times in life I have wondered whether it is better to be ordered about from pillar to post or to stay put in the place of one's choice. If, in the long run, only character counts, it may not be an asset to develop a chameleon power of adaptation to environment. For years past it has been my lot to move about the world at the bidding of unseen powers, in other words to follow the drum. Called on to make a home sometimes in Germany or America, at other times in England or Ireland, it is inevitable that some vistas appeared less inviting than others. When an assignment to Durham came, my heart sank, for I remembered the slag-heaps, chimneys, derricks, and blocks of houses on black moors glimpsed from train windows, and the prospect of passing four winters and four summers in so defaced a landscape did not at first present itself in an alluring light. Had I known that to the people who inhabit these northern regions, England south of the Trent was regarded as a negligible, parasitic district of baker's bread and niminy-piminy ways, I might have felt real discouragement. It was soon impressed on me that the men of the north bore the world on their shoulders, that they forged steel, hewed coal, built ships and, unlike the folk of the south, were no hucksterers of manufactured goods. They could boast of bridging tropical rivers in Africa, of constructing

engines that would climb the slopes of the Andes.
Whenever my train drew into Darlington I was reminded of these claims, for from my carriage window
I could see the bones of a metal megatherium with the
word "Zambesi" chalked upon its side, mute witness
to the power of the north.

In order to re-establish a sense of identity which
every change of habitation submerges, once settled in
Durham I began to cast about for a means of self-
integration.   What could I do to escape the impact of
condor circumstance?   The necessity of squeezing an
advantage from the situation by attaching myself to
some local concern imposed itself upon me.

Sir Walter Scott at the end of the eighteenth century
had found Northumbria a place after his own heart.
Would it be possible, I wondered, to walk in the foot-
steps of this first popularizer of archæology and enjoy
as he did exploring the Wall, the feudal castles, the
monastic houses and the fortress cathedral of Durham?
Archæology seemed to be the passion of the north and
the love of antiquarian things almost universal.   It was
easy enough to get hold of information and to plan
excursions.   Many happy days were spent investigating the stone relics of the past, and of all sights the
tiny church of the Venerable Bede on its mud estuary
at Jarrow touched me most.   Jervaulx, Rievaulx,
Fountains, Mount Grace, Middleton, Barnard Castle,
Raby, Bolton, I visited all these and many more only
in the end to realize that my delightful wanderings led
me into a blind alley, the path to which had been taped
and explored by countless clergymen and schoolmasters

whose interest stopped dead as it seemed with the Reformation or the Stuart dynasty. The ruins in which members of archæological clubs took their pleasure were the remnants of distant centuries and the expression of an extinct way of life that seemed to have no bearing whatever on the present. Between those days and these lay a sundering morass of years. When for a variety of reasons such buildings had fallen out of use, English life had not come to a halt. It had pulsed vigorously on in other forms, but what forms? What was there to show, for example, for the generations that had passed between the Cromwellian and Victorian eras? Could it all be summed up architecturally in places of worship, alms-houses, and country seats? Were there really no other clues, visible or invisible, to the life in between?

One day business took us to Seaham, to the Vane-Tempest pit set in once verdant country, now broken in contour to retrieve the coal on which the fortunes of the local landlords depended. I asked myself what it could have looked like before the advent of the industrial revolution that sent men scampering from the sunny fields to the lightless galleries? How had it struck Byron, for example? Business done, we wandered on to Seaham House, the former home of the Milbankes and the scene of the poet's marriage. I found myself face to face with the ghost of an eighteenth-century villa set on a cliff fenced about with Italianate balustrades, terraces, and lawns, a ghost-house that had been incongruously endowed with a new body of brick annexes and open wards to fit it for the tuberculous patients of a County Sanatorium. In a flash I knew what it was that needed doing. The literary associations of the county of Durham must somehow be preserved if only to lay away in lavender. Never far below the surface of my mind are the lines of a poem read to me by W. B. Yeats many years ago in Lady Gregory's library at Coole. I can still hear the sonorous chanting tones of that unique voice:

> Of all the many painted things
> In dreary dancing past far whirled
> *Words alone are certain good.*

Into Seaham House, this private setting for private life now adapted for a communal purpose, I read a warning and a lesson. The writing on Belshazzar's wall was not more plain. A warning that if I did not make haste there would be not only no records, but no houses ghost-like or otherwise to tell me their story. A lesson that the day for personal possessing was over, that de-individualization was to be the fate of houses and of men, that England was being communized without a revolution.

Once this notion entered my head it acted potently. Everywhere I went I saw things happening that strengthened my conviction that it was almost too late to rescue memories of the kind I had in mind. Not only had moorland valleys been converted into reservoirs for distant cities, and rivers, which had once held salmon, been polluted by chemicals, but the eighteenth-century houses themselves were actually dissolving under one's eyes as I had seen them doing in Russia.

They were not actually labelled, as the gardens of crumbling palaces in Leningrad are labelled, "Park of Rest and Culture," but they are tottering on the same incline. Windlestone, the Edens' home, serving as a hostel for tramps, Hardwick demesne turned over, serpentine, temples, and all, to unemployed men. A kind of panic seized me as I motored along the ever-extending ribbon roads, past flimsy Council cots that gave the effect of a moving belt of hutches. Where was this tentacular urbanization to stop? Was I assisting at the obliteration of tradition only or at the foundering of the social structure in which I had been reared? Was a social revolution being carried out in this quiet unrevolutionary way?

If there is one thing more terrifying than another in this world it is the bevy of thinkers who loom portentous behind the scene. What did Wellington or his contemporaries know of the retiring officer, Clausewitz, who, in the peace that followed Waterloo, hammered out the concepts of war that made Germany the dominant military power of 1870? What did Queen Victoria know of the burly, bearded Jew who sat cogitating on Primrose Hill while she was holding decorous Drawing-rooms at Buckingham Palace? And yet it was Karl Marx and not Queen Victoria and her Empire builders, who was planning the new world. The two books these Germans wrote, on War and on Capital, turned the world upside-down. They were implemented some time ago by a third German book, *My Fight*, which has worked like the others by a kind of delayed action and has proved as dynamic as its predecessors. The cumulative impact of these mental torpedoes on the mind of European man has resulted in a form of mechanized activity that threatens to speed up the disintegration of society as we know it. One asks oneself whether the past must be utterly destroyed and if anything of the old fragile contemplative life can be salvaged and preserved or must all disappear in the onrush of a material socialism that seems to be the negation of the intellectual and spiritual values.

* * * * *

Obviously there was no time to lose. I must collect local lore and seek out the places that might yield the memories. Undeterred by occasional rebuffs from local residents such as "What does Byron matter? He is a very over-rated poet." "I don't believe Coleridge ever set foot in Durham," or "You are *quite* wrong, Wordsworth did not live at Sockburn," or "Nobody knows anything about the author of Jorrocks, *Handley Cross* is good fun, but what *does* the author matter?" I plodded on. The results of my investigations are in this volume.

I poked about in lanes leading to nowhere, walked amongst wild flowers in untrodden brakes and by river reaches which fishermen have reluctantly abandoned and got to know every corner of the countryside. Living as I do with one foot in the nineteenth century and the other in the twentieth, I encouraged myself by thinking that to record a past, which though not distant was already half forgotten, would take me back

into an England unelectrified and staid. My immediate surroundings now took on for me a different
aspect: Durham was no longer a mere network of coalfields, but a Tom Tiddler's ground of memory. Anywhere might I light on a glittering trail, and even when
visiting engineering works, camps, shipbuilding yards,
and armament factories, I could hug to my soul the
thought that just round the corner within sight of the
smoke palls and within sound of the sirens lay significant vales of quietness where poets had once paced
the grass in meditation and where one might still gather
oxlips and hear the linnet sing.

The life of a hundred or a hundred and fifty years
ago is altogether more perishable than that embodied
in the buildings of the preceding centuries. Again
and again I asked myself: "Is there really nothing to
show for the eighteenth and nineteenth centuries save
country-houses characterizing a phase of culture that
is in process of being engulfed by the tide of public
advancement?" When so much else had gone by the
board, was it any use seeking for something so intangible
as the places connected with men of letters? And yet
if only I could gather what there was still to gather I
should be preserving a fraction of the traditional life
of England, something as traditional, let us say, as the
story of the feudal lords, abbots, and country gentry
now gone into an historic or economic discard. In a
sense, the influence of men of letters is more potent
than any of these forces for they have the universal
quality in their appeal. Wordsworth's Sonnets, for
example, have been read by Englishmen the world over

and have been accepted by Chinese nature-lovers as our peculiar contribution to the essential wealth of the world. In verse, the English spirit is inviolate, as inviolate as it is in water-colour landscape. No imprint of their sojourn on building or monument has been left by poets and writers, they have usually been too poor for that, but they have associated themselves intimately, and indelibly, in their passage through life with certain fields, certain rivers, and certain houses. Rather unreasonably, perhaps, the places loved by authors assume for me a special lustre analogous to the "glory" of religious art, and I feel strongly that what has pertained to the life of the mind or spirit must not be permitted by indifference to fall out of remembrance.

With great satisfaction I assured myself by reading that the north had once been the haunt of poets and the nursery of prose writers. Instead of the ribbon roads I began to see in the mind's eye the old turnpikes travelled by Scott, Southey, Dickens, and Shelley. It was in this now denatured countryside that Byron and Wordsworth had conducted their courtships, in this part of the world they had been married. Scott had walked on Greta banks and Coleridge by Tees. Southey had conversed with John Lingard at Ushaw and Dickens had found a title for a book at Barnard Castle. And as for the natives of the district, Robert Surtees and Robert Smith Surtees, could they not of themselves lift the county above the rising tide of anonymous productivity, and cause the name of Durham to ring round the world?

The knowledge that these men of letters had once

18

lived in the county in which I was a temporary dweller gave me all the impetus I needed to pursue my quest.

> Communities are lost, and Empires die,
> And things of holy use unhallowed lie;
> They perish;—but the Intellect can raise,
> From airy words alone, a Pile that ne'er decays.

If words could raise a cairn to the poets and writers who once had lived in Durham County I would contribute my stone.

THE BYRONS AT SEAHAM

THE BYRONS AT SEAHAM

I n the beginning of my quest, luck favoured me, for one day when having tea in a neighbouring country house I was handed a drawer full of papers to look through. "You're interested in that sort of thing, I know," observed my hostess. "I think all the papers are at least a hundred years old and that some of them are about Byron. Aren't you a Byron fan?" I smiled assent to this indictment, for I had read every letter and every life of Byron and at the time had serious thoughts of writing a book to show how much better I understood him than anyone else, a feeling that I believe I share with many members of my sex. Yes, I could honestly call myself a Byron fan.

The papers in the drawer were in no particular order, some were tied into bundles with tape, others were in envelopes, others loose. A sheet of newspaper was spread on the broad sofa beside me and I was allowed to turn the drawer out, the better to investigate its contents. As I did so there rolled on to the carpet a little object. I retrieved it; it was a thimble. My heart gave a leap, could it, oh could it be the thimble for which Byron had dived into the Greet at the bidding of Elizabeth Pigot? The envelope from which it had fallen presently came to my hand: it was endorsed with the words, "Thimble belonging to Miss Elizabeth Pigot. It was thrown into the river Greet and three times the poet Lord Byron dived in and brought it up." I gloated over the treasure-trove and with rising excitement opened another envelope. It contained a pair of folding scissors which, according to the super-scription, Lord Byron had kept in his pocket for trimming his nails. They had been acquired after his death by his valet, Fletcher, as a souvenir, and at Fletcher's death had found their way into the keeping of Miss Pigot, by then an old woman. Next I came on a pen-and-ink sketch initialled 'E.P. 1806,' bearing the legend, "The house in which Lord Byron resided on Burgage Green, Southwell, when he first printed his poems." I noticed that all the windows of the little Georgian dwelling were shut except that of Lord Byron's bedroom. Another larger drawing lay under-neath this sketch, a careful pencil drawing of the south elevation of Seaham House dated 1815. It had been made by a schoolmaster who had walked the cliff road from Sunderland to Hartlepool in February that year, that is, as I at once realized, four or five weeks after the Byron-Milbanke marriage. The wedding was still the great topic of conversation in the village, and as the stranger got talking he heard all about 'Miss Nancy,' everyone had known her since she was a baby. It was surely strange that she should choose a lord from the south; but young maids were all alike and would always fall for a handsome man, and the bride-groom was certainly handsome. They had hoped for the usual wedding junketings, but there had been no entertaining, no health drinking, no wedding guests, even neighbours and relations had not been invited.

SEAHAM HOUSE, FEBRUARY 1815

A cross indicates the room in which the wedding took place

It had been a queer business, and though the church was so close to the house, right on the lawn, as one might say, the marriage had taken place in the drawing-room.

The schoolmaster was young, he had read *Childe Harold* and was an enthusiast for the new autobiographical mode in poetry, it was up to date, and all unlike the hoary chivalry of Scott's rhymed romances. Byron understood men's hearts and men's passions, he understood the sea and he understood love. To the schoolmaster he seemed a demi-god. To think that this great poet had just been married in this very place. Was it any way possible for him to have a look at the house and perhaps see the windows of the room in which the ceremony had been celebrated? They told him he could go up the dene as far as the bottom of the garden, he would be hidden from observation there and could have as long a look as he liked. Gladly he went and gallantly he tried to make a sketch of the house (it must have been done with a ruler) in memory of his visit. It was unlikely that he would ever get nearer to his idol than that, but even that would be a precious link. Though no artist, as we may see, he managed to preserve a record of the building that had been the scene of what he figured as a highly significant event. To me his drawing was more than a link, it was a miraculous passport into the vanished world I had set myself to explore.

Enheartened by these finds, I borrowed the pencil drawing, the ink sketch, the thimble, and the scissors from my hostess and had them all photographed. I

then took the photograph of the drawing over to Seaham to compare it with the present building, and found
that the eighteenth-century villa, though large, had
been a far plainer structure than Seaham House, for it
had been unadorned with the copings and balustrades
imposed on it by the taste of later occupants. Set on
a cliff overlooking the German Ocean and, save for
screen plantations, exposed to all the winds of heaven,
I knew that to Lord Byron's bride it had been a most
cherished home. In contrast to the elevated position
of the big house, the adjacent fishing village, like many
other house-clusters along the Northumbrian coast,
nestled snugly by the shore at the point where the fresh
water issued from the small ravine or dene which, passing earlier in its course through the grounds of Seaham
House, formed the owners' only refuge from the wind.
Walking down to the dene I found myself on a path, the
path paced by Byron on his wedding morning. He
had always hated wind, it made him restless and unhappy, and the old woman, who showed me round the
kitchen garden knowing that, had pointed out to me
the gooseberry border by the wall, where he had also
sheltered and the road beyond with its patulous sycamores. From the cliff edge I was made to look at the
Featherbed Rocks jutting up from the wet sand as the
point to which Miss Nancy took her lame bridegroom
to enjoy the sea breezes; but had he cared about sea-
breezes? It was thought not; he had come from
London and southerners were soft.

* * * * *

26

It was to Seaham House that Ralph Milbanke in 1777 had brought his young wife, Judith Noel. In those more candid days there were no coal-pits or belching chimneys to smirch air or field, and the county of Durham, except for its commercial centres and its ports, was a completely rural area sprinkled with villages and country seats. During the summer months, when those with political interests or Court appointments moved to London, the country was at its quietest, but during autumn it developed great social activity. Big landowners opened their houses for hunt breakfasts and shooting-parties and by night diverted their guests with gambling and theatricals. Hunt balls, a prominent feature of winter gaieties, took place in the market towns of the various districts and thereat county society, as yet compact, exclusive, and un-threatened by the invasion of industrialists, danced, since English music was unprocurable, to the tunes played by foreign musicians.

For years Mr. and Mrs. Ralph Milbanke spent the greater part of their time at Seaham, moving, however, for the worst of the winter gales to Elemore, near Durham, the home of their cousins, the George Bakers. Compared with the villa on the cliff, Elemore, which was but six miles inland, was warm and sheltered; woodcock lighted in the woods and duck on the lake near the garden. In this fine Cromwellian house it was possible to avoid the tempestuous weather and enjoy good sport on two or three days of the week.

Seaham House being partially unfurnished and in use as a sanatorium, I found it was to Elemore one

27

should look for traces of the Milbankes and their ways, so to Elemore I went. The house is still very much as it was a hundred and fifty years ago and preserves on its elegant library shelves books that must have been fingered both by Byron and the Milbanke family. At Elemore I was shown rooms set apart for Milbanke occupation, doors labelled with their names, blankets tagged for their beds, linen tablecloths woven, it is said, of flax of Judith Milbanke's spinning, and quilts and cushions stitched by her in hexagon patchwork. Mrs. Milbanke, who followed hounds regularly and walked with the guns, included among her indoor tastes reading and music. She accompanied her husband's voice on the harpsichord and also his violin, as he was fond of fiddling in the evenings. Her commonplace books seem to betray a latent romanticism, for in them we find transcribed the early poems of her future son-in-law. I got the impression that Judith Milbanke had been a cheerful person making the best of a life that she was careful to inform her daughter in later years had been "no Bed of Roses." Ralph Milbanke appears to have been a joke-cracking nonentity and was portrayed by Sir Joshua Reynolds as a very personable country gentleman. Husband and wife were good companions, and none the less so for sharing for thirteen years a common disappointment, that of childlessness. In the beginning they had longed for a nursery of their own, then when hope seemed vain and Judith's sister, Mrs. Nathaniel Curzon, died in 1782, they took the motherless little girl into their house at Seaham and life jogged on as before, though perhaps more contentedly. Its even tenour was interrupted when Ralph Milbanke was lifted out of private life into public affairs by being returned to the House of Commons as member for Durham County at the General Election of 1790. The change involved residence in London for the summer session, and expensive and sometimes sudden calls at other times to vote on special occasions. The sort of income that sufficed for country life did not go far in a constituency, with the result that, during the twenty-two years he sat in Parliament, Ralph Milbanke spent most of his capital and mortgaged his Seaham property. Expenditure of this kind he took rather lightly, since both he and his wife had expectations. As heir to a baronetcy and the estate of Halnaby, and as husband of a woman who must one day inherit the Noel fortune from her brother, Lord Wentworth, he was beyond fear of destitution.

Than a London house Mrs. Milbanke asked nothing better, since it enabled her to satisfy all her latent blue-stocking tendencies by setting up a little *salon* in which Sarah Siddons, Joanna Baillie, and Maria Edgeworth appeared as stars, and though she could in no way compete with the important and comprehensive entertaining of her sister-in-law, Lady Melbourne, she too could shine in her own corner and in her own way. The year after this improvement in fortune she became surprisingly and joyfully aware that she was going to have a child, though after fourteen barren years the prospect seemed almost unbelievable. She was staying at Elemore at the time and there was no question in her mind but that this comfortable house, so close to good Dr.

Bainbridge of Durham, must be the scene of the birth rather than their own windswept villa by the sea. The Bakers acquiescing in the plan, the Milbankes made Elemore their home till Ascension Day, 1792, when a baby girl was born to them. The welcome extended to the tiny new-comer was intensified by long adjournment to ecstasy. What could it matter that it was a girl and not a boy? What, indeed, did anything matter to the parents except that they had been gifted with the loveliest baby that anyone had ever seen? It might well have been presumed that a child born in such happy circumstances might count on enjoying more than twenty-two years of happiness out of a lifetime of sixty-eight years. Yet somehow a destiny that obviously lay in the direction of making a conventional marriage with some country gentleman was frustrated by a self-willed girl who, when she had the chance, snatched at the unknown and the mysterious. She certainly could not have been intended by nature for the wife of a genius.

England in the summer of 1792 was quiet enough, though deeply stirred by the news from France. Soon after their baby's birth the Milbankes read of the imprisonment of Louis XVI and later again of the proclamation of a Republic. Paris in those days seemed a long way off and the Milbankes when they drove over to Seaham were too engrossed installing their "Nancy" in her nursery to worry much about foreign troubles. Solicitously they watched over the growth of their treasure. Presently little Sophy Curzon was to help the baby to toddle up and down green slopes and rock-flecked sands, and a kind of nursery governess, Mrs. Clermont, was engaged to preside over the child's upbringing and general deportment. When Nancy was six and Sophy sixteen Ralph Milbanke inherited, through the death of his father, Sir Mark, the fine house and estate known as Halnaby Hall, forty miles away on the south bank of the Tees and therefore just outside the county of Durham. No one was less pleased with the inheritance than Nancy, who found herself whisked away from the seashore and set down in the middle of a large green park. Halnaby as she grew older seemed to her far duller than Seaham and not so beautiful as Elemore.

The early marriage of her cousin Sophy to Lord Tamworth in 1800 left Nancy very much alone and at the mercy of her own zeal for acquiring knowledge. Far too eagerly did she absorb the teaching of the local schoolmaster and therethrough develop a strong taste for mathematics. This had the rather unfortunate effect of inculcating in her a quality of cool appraisement and objective judgment that made her so impossible a wife for a temperamental man. Never did a girl come into the world who would have profited more from learning the couplet,

> Leave all thy pedant lore apart
> God hid the whole world in thy heart,

than Nancy, who early came to conceal and even stifle feelings that would have been far better released. Lady Byron has been described by one biographer as a high-flown romantic; by another as a self-forgetting

31

sentimentalist. Neither of these descriptions really fits her as a girl, and the girl may be said to be the mother of the woman. We have only to look at the list of books owned by Miss Milbanke to realize at once that her natural taste leaned neither to literature nor to romance. Mathematics, Logarithms, Euclid, Mensuration, Conic Sections, to begin with: Suetonius, Cæsar, Tacitus, to go on with, and these books were her preferred and daily fare. Surely here is indication enough of scientific inclination and an obvious preference of matters of fact over matters of fancy. Sophy Tamworth used to say that her cousin Annabella had "superior intellects"; even her doting mother remarked that she was "too superior for common life"; and it may even be, as Emerson once sententiously suggested, that "intellect tends to void itself of affection."

In fairness one has to mention the fact that volumes of Ossian and Gray also stood on her shelves, but they may have been gifts and were obviously secondary to the main interests. The girl was given a boy's mental training, and it would not surprise one to learn that in the process she had caught the trick of so controlling her emotional reactions as to find herself later in life baulked, by layers of repressions, of any outlet for the natural simpler feelings of girlhood. If it really was her destiny to marry a romantic, one is inclined to think that no education at all would have been better than the particular education she received.

At Halnaby, as child of the Hall, Miss Nancy assumed greater importance than at Seaham, and of necessity became an object of special interest to both

villagers and tenant farmers. Circumstances tended
to swell her idea of herself as one apart from common
things. A visit to London in the year of the Peace of
Amiens (1802) turned out to be memorable, for she
was painted by Hoppner as a pretty rosy-cheeked child
in a muslin dress giving the effect of prolonged infancy.
It is easy to read into this picture all the sentiment of
parents who, having become possessed of a baby in
middle life, never wanted it to grow up. Quite un-
avoidably Nancy was adored and swamped in solici-
tude; quite naturally this had the result of forcing her
to a kind of secret reserve within herself. The fetters
of gossamer that allowed her to ride, but not to tire
herself, to walk with the guns, but not too far, to watch
the salmon-fishing in the Tees, but not to get chilled,
were physically unescapable, but even though restraint
and circumspection were early drilled into her she was
always one for having her own way and was not by
nature docile. Trained, as all little girls belonging to
Halls in those days were trained, to set an example to
the village children, on Sundays she walked through
Croft with her parents, meeting lock-pulling, curtseying
folk, entered the church and climbed demurely, and
maybe self-consciously, up the wide balustered stair
leading to the grand Halnaby pew, the pew that owing
to its ornate structure looks to us so much more like
an opera-box than a retreat for prayer.

Had this well-drilled child the time or the chance to
play the make-believe games of childhood and escape
into fairyland? Was the rein ever slacked for instinctive life or was a kind of strait-waistcoat character im-

posed upon her? Perhaps it was inevitable she should grow up that way, but to set oneself over against things in cool detachment is not part of the make-up of adolescence, which hurls itself passionately from one emotion or enthusiasm to the next. It is not natural to calculate and to reflect before every action. And yet such training fitted in all too well with the original inclination to be matter-of-fact. In the end it was this very capacity for reflexion that was her undoing; she depended too much on the head, too little on the heart, and when faced by dilemmas that were in themselves abnormal and with action the result of which must be unpredictable she still behaved as though confronted by a mathematical problem and in inexperienced self-sufficiency blundered to what seemed to her a rational solution. It is doubtful whether she learnt, even by bitter experience, how irrational life can be.

*　　*　　*　　*　　*

Sir Ralph ceased to play any part in politics just at the time Annabella should have come out and announced that he would not stand at the next Election. Judging himself too poor to give her a London season, he made no arrangement to introduce his daughter at Court till the spring of the year 1811, when she was sent to stay in Great Cumberland Place for the season under the chaperonage of her young friend Lady Gosford.

It was rather a disadvantage to come out at nineteen and Annabella found herself assessed by her contemporaries, who had most of them been out two seasons, as a little stiff in manner and perhaps not so very amusing. Though it really took time to find one's London feet and learn to be light in hand, she wrote home to her parents as if she were completely mistress of the situation and somewhat of a despiser of frivolities. The parents, who of course doted on her letters, learned that she had extracted no pleasure from a visit to the Opera with Aunt Melbourne. To one who "neither cared about flirting" or "listening to squalling" it was merely a fatiguing experience. She declared herself "not to be absorbed in the present scene," and her mother and father wondered rather wistfully why she was not enjoying herself light-heartedly and as a young girl should. Her letters to them seemed just a little grand and just a shade disappointing. Having given her her head for four months, Sir Ralph and Lady Milbanke went to London in July to fetch her home to Seaham, where she had plenty of time on her hands to realize how much she missed the despised merry-go-round. How dull were the neighbours! Who of them had read *Madoc* and who *Evelina*? With whom could one discuss new books and poetry? Even the cobbler poet of Seaham, Joe Blackett, was dead. As dust in her mouth were the compliments of country gentlemen satisfied with their rusticity. After a winter spent with her rapidly ageing parents (Sir Ralph was 65 and her mother 62) playing chess and commerce, and mildly following Lord Darlington's hounds, she planned an escape to London. Return she must, for was not Fate lurking for her in the purlieus of Whitehall?

35

As Sir Ralph and Lady Milbanke could not afford to take her to London themselves before Easter (1812), they begged her to stay in the country with them till May, but she insisted on joining Lady Gosford again in February. Letters from every coach-halt on the London road revealed not only that her appetite for her favourite food, mutton chops, was extremely good, but that her joy in escape from what she called "the dullities of Seaham" made her brim over with jocularity.

Annabella's second season proved far more agreeable than her first, for she was no longer shy and she knew a good many people. In spite of the fact that her tastes remained serious, that she frequented the British Museum, attended Mr. Thomas Campbell's lectures at the Royal Institution, and took notes at classes on Mnemonics and Geology, she was able to assure her family that she was "quite the fashion"—in other words, that she was asked everywhere. A satisfactory number of beaux were reported to Seaham, and under this heading the devoted parents heard of Lord Jocelyn, Treasurer to the Prince Regent; William Bankes, with eight thousand a year; George Eden, a country neighbour; General Pakenham, back from the Peninsula; Augustus Foster, son of Elizabeth Duchess of Devonshire; and we may take it that anyone of these gentlemen would have been more likely to have made her happy than the man she was later to insist on marrying.

What Annabella looked like at this time is shown in the miniature made by Sir George Hayter, commissioned at £20 by fond, proud parents who told each other that they could not hope to keep their precious attractive girl at home much longer. All too soon must they resign themselves to welcome a satisfactory son-in-law into the family. It did not occur to them that they might be called on to put up with one who was not satisfactory.

Lady Milbanke had by this time developed an enthusiastic admiration for Lord Byron 'and all his works. Nancy, who had not so far made his acquaintance, did not share her mother's interest in acquiring an early copy of *Childe Harold* (due for publication on March 10th, 1812), but when dining at Melbourne House five days after it had appeared she heard the new work and its author discussed. Everyone was excited by the intensely personal nature of the narrative, and Caro Lamb, having hurriedly read the advance copy lent her by Samuel Rogers, praised it vociferously. Her cousin, Annabella, disdained the excited chatter and resolved not to look at the book for "at least a week." Principles must be adhered to, and it was against hers to give way to any impulse, far less any prevailing *furore*. When at last she did open the volume she entered in her diary the not very apt remarks that "the author was a mannerist" and the poem "reminiscent of *Vathek*." The day after penning this entry Annabella attended Caro Lamb's waltzing class at Melbourne House and for the first time clapped eyes on the poet. Byron, as she informed her parents, was on this occasion "the object of universal attention" and "of course Lady C. had seized on him!" From her diary we gather that she set herself to watch Byron with particular care. From his mouth, which he covered with his hand, was to be deduced "acrimony of spirit," from his upper lip, drawn towards the nose, "impatient disgust": his lips, she noted, "thickened with disdain," "his eyes rolled impatiently." Could he, she wondered, be spiritually in sympathy with her and as contemptuous of the giddy scene as she was? What donkeys the women of her set were to pay court to such a creature! They ought to know that their behaviour would "only earn the lash of his satire."

Amusing though it might be to be the unnoticed observer of Lord Byron at a waltz class, it was by no means so amusing to be ignored at Lady Gosford's rout, where Lord Byron was the most sought-after guest. To be domiciled, as Annabella was, in the house of a great friend, present from the beginning to the end of a party, and not to have introduced to her the lion of the evening, was really mortifying, more especially as she had promised herself to give Mamma the story of a first-hand encounter.

As luck would have it, the very day after the Gosford rout she was due to be taken to a supper-party at her cousin, Lady Cowper's house. Mrs. George Lamb was her chaperon and on this occasion Lord Byron was presented to her. She at once spoke to him of her *protégé*, the cobbler poet of Seaham, to whom the author had alluded a little ungenerously in *English Bards and Scotch Reviewers*. Did Lord Byron know that the poor fellow had died the previous year on the Seaham estate? This was quite a satisfactory interview to write home about. She had been Joe Blackett's patron, Byron his detractor, yet Byron had shown himself deferential and willing to be converted. "He is very handsome," she informed Mamma, "his manners are in a superior degree, such as one would attribute to Nature's gentleman," and again after another party she wrote, "Lord Byron is without exception, young or old, more agreeable in conversation than any person I ever knew."

One day towards the end of April, Caro Lamb had at the author's request shown to Lord Byron the poems her cousin Annabella had composed at Seaham. He had judged them pretty, smooth, and improvable by slight alterations, and better, much better, than anything written by "that poor dead dunce of a Cobbler-Laureat." He had added, evidently in reply to some question of Lady Caroline's, that he had no desire to be more closely acquainted with Miss Milbanke. It was possible that he "might like her more if she were less perfect," but she might be "too good for a fallen spirit to know."

Caro derived malicious enjoyment from imparting these opinions to her cousin. The poor girl was a prig, but could she really be such a prig as to delude herself into the belief that Lord Byron admired her? The letter she had read aloud should teach her better than that. Why could not Annabella be satisfied with the partner rumour had allotted to her, George Eden, who from a family point of view was an entirely suitable match? Why must she come nosing into other people's preserves? Was Annabella, and at this point she spoke directly, was Annabella thinking of becoming engaged to George Eden? Annabella denied that she had thought of such a match, and when she got home made the entry in her diary that she had "undeceived Lady Caroline by a painful acknowledgment."

*　　*　　*　　*　　*

More and more curious did Miss Milbanke become about the romantic Childe: was he really as enigmatic a character as people liked to make out? Was he lonely? Was he unhappy? Was he in need of a good woman's love? Had he really no friends, as he said, and if so, why was he so constantly with Aunt Elizabeth at Melbourne House? And why did he dance attendance on Caro? His character began to assume the interest and complexity of a difficult mathematical problem. He was certainly unlike the young men she knew in Durham and unlike the young men she was meeting at London parties. He seemed older than his twenty-four years and more experienced than anyone she knew. Perhaps, but she hardly formulated the idea as yet, it was her rôle to be the perfect friend, the friend he said he had never found. She thought herself into a state of benignancy towards the lonely creature and as the result of much cogitation intimated to her parents that she would "consider it an act of humanity and a Christian duty not to deny him any temporary satisfaction he can derive from my acquaintance—though I shall not seek to increase it. He is not a dangerous person to me." The letter, though rather fatuous in expression, startled her parents. Down came Sir Ralph and Lady Milbanke to London, for they felt the urgency of finding out for themselves whether their pet was making a fool of herself or not. Both were only too well aware of the kind of madness that Byron had inspired in Caro Lamb. Elizabeth Melbourne had told them all about it. What could their child mean by "temporary satisfaction" or any similar nonsense? The arrival of her parents in London put an effectual stop to further experiments on Annabella's part and the rest of the season spent under the close chaperonage of father and mother proved very dull. No further opportunity offered itself of talks with the romantic Childe and therefore the analysis of his most intriguing character could not be proceeded with. When the Milbankes reached home Annabella looked back a little wistfully on the balls and the routs and the dinners. How little she had to show for all the social activities, could she even be sure that she had riveted Lord Byron's interest?

In many a walk beside the sea the girl raked over her London experiences. Lord Byron had certainly shown her attention, but then he appeared to pay attention to a number of women, and not least to her aunt, Elizabeth Melbourne. In spite of the difference in age, it was a great friendship; how great those who come after know better than Annabella, though even Annabella realized how heavily the Childe leaned on her father's sister for counsel and sympathy. They seemed to understand each other very well. What advice was Aunt Melbourne giving to Byron about marriage? Was she in favour of his settling down with some suitable girl or would she rather he remained unmarried?

If Annabella could have read a letter written in September (1812) by her aunt enquiring of Byron whether he is *sure* that he wishes to marry her niece, some of her questions would have answered themselves. From his reply we may assume that the matter had been discussed between them: "You ask me whether I am *sure* of myself, and I answer, *No*, but you are, which I take to be a much better thing." So Lady Melbourne had recommended Annabella as a suitable wife! Maybe this advice was the outcome of leisured talks at Cheltenham Spa, where Society had that autumn gathered to drink the waters. The Melbournes were there and the Jerseys and the Oxfords, and, of course, that sufferer from stone, Lord Byron. The result of the talks was that a proposal of marriage was made by Lady Melbourne to her niece on behalf of Lord Byron. Byron evidently intended her to try and find out how the land lay and later on said his friend had exceeded her instructions; he had merely wished her to explore his chances of being accepted but not to make a serious proposal of marriage. It is obvious he did not see the actual letter.

The letter reached Annabella at Richmond in Yorkshire and apparently did not thrill her in the way one would have expected. She weighed the proposal in a business-like way, and it is open to doubt whether she told her parents anything about the substance of her aunt's letter. After careful appraisement of her suitor's character she sat down a day or two later to inform Aunt Melbourne that the person on whose behalf she had written could "never be the object of that strong affection which would make me happy in domestic life." How wryly must the recipient of this communication have smiled at the priggishness of the reply. When told that he had failed in his proxy courtship the rejected suitor showed no signs of chagrin, saying lightly that his heart had never had an opportunity of being much interested in the business. As a matter of fact, Byron was in the thick of his love-affair with Lady Oxford and could pay attention to little else. Undiscouraged by her niece's behaviour, which she regarded as attitudinizing, Lady Melbourne told the girl "to get off her stilts" and, anticipating Oscar Wilde, suggested that she might be given an idea of what in her niece's opinion would constitute "an ideal husband." Nothing loath, Annabella drew up a list of indispensable qualities, among which was "an equal tenor of affection towards me, *not* violent affection." In thus ruling out all passionate complications the girl was certainly betraying a greater simplicity than might have been expected after two London seasons. It is rather surprising, in a way, to find Lady Melbourne continuing to take an interest in her niece's character, but the explanation probably lies in the fact that she had time to waste at Cheltenham Spa and was aggravated by Byron's blatant infatuation with Lady Oxford. Associating, as she was, with the Jerseys, the Hollands, and the Cowpers, she felt in a greater degree than they, though all were interested, that a suitable marriage should be arranged without delay for this peccable, handsome young man. He had done a good deal of destructive work in his twenty-four years. Is it permissible to suggest that at this time the poet was the victim of a gynocratic conspiracy to safeguard society? From time to time he had told them one and all that he believed a wife would be his salvation. But how he of all men the least tameable, a man who looked to women for relaxation and adored in them the unforeseen and the spontaneous, could ever have been shepherded into marriage with a girl without variety and without the gift of self-expression must remain an enigma.

* * * * *

The winter of 1812–13 was passed by the Milbankes at Halnaby. It was very cold and to Annabella oppressively dull. County neighbours, meets of hounds, shooting-parties had all lost their savour, and the more Annabella was thrown back on country pursuits the less happiness she found in them. Her real life, her personal life, lay, she was persuaded, in books, in learning, in associating with distinguished persons. London could give her all she needed, in London alone could she fulfil her destiny.

Despite falling funds and family debts, Miss Milbanke managed to drag her parents up to Mayfair again for a third season, that of 1813. There she had the interest of watching Byron at parties and seeing him run after by everyone she knew, but there was no bridging of the ditch she had dug between herself and him by her refusal of his offer of marriage. They did not so much as exchange words during the weeks the Milbankes were in London.

There was a great deal of gaiety, for people were in good heart over the victory of Leipzig and believed the end of the long wars was in sight. The star among the foreign visitors was Madame de Staël. Byron was greatly taken up with her and constantly at the Hollands' and the Jerseys'. From Annabella's point of view the season was a shattering disappointment, nothing happened to redeem the want of success. In July the Milbanke family returned to Seaham for the rest of the warm weather.

*   *   *   *   *

Once more Miss Milbanke tramped the Seaham sands, once more went over her experiences in London and quite inevitably her thoughts centred round the part played by her clever aunt in trying to shape her course. After all, Aunt Elizabeth had herself once been a young girl living at Halnaby and going to Seaham, leading precisely the life she was leading at the moment, but her aunt had extricated herself, had married, cut adrift from "dullities" and carved out for herself the most interesting of lives. Was marriage also to be her way out? Was it for her the only way out? If it was, what was to hinder her from imitating her aunt, was she not of age and could she not twist her parents round her finger? Was it possible that her experienced and clever relation might have displayed superior judgment when she tried to arrange a match for her with Lord Byron? What was now to be read into her aunt's letters? Did they not show that she clung to the idea that the young people might still come together? Had she not owned to passing on messages expressing her niece's constant interest in his doings? Might it not be advisable to follow this up? What if she wrote direct to Lord Byron and managed to insinuate into her letter something to show how deep and faithful was her concern. Conundrums of this sort wrecked Annabella's peace of mind. After oscillating for two or three weeks between action and inaction her mind snapped suddenly down on to the decision to stake all on explaining herself to the Childe. Sitting at her writing-table one hot August morning, she began to compose one of the longest and it must be owned one of the most pompous letters ever penned, its excuse being a desire to assure Lord Byron that she was his true friend. She told him that he had once commented on the serenity of her countenance; she might appear serene, but she could suffer as deeply as he had suffered. The letter was not only a request for friendship but a plea for a better understanding. She states that her parents are in her confidence (one wonders whether this could be true?) but on no account must Lady Melbourne be allowed to get wind of the correspondence.

The letter was opened by Byron in his Bennet Street rooms, which at the moment were echoing with the laughter of his half-sister Augusta Leigh. Funny Augusta, the Gussy and sometimes Goosey, who always put him in conceit with himself, who saw nothing wrong in anything and who had already spent six weeks in his company. Not too much engrossed by Goosey to reply, Byron wrote to inform Miss Milbanke that he really cannot believe himself to be the friend she is seeking and then rather good-humouredly adds, "I doubt whether I could help loving you." The correspondence thus inaugurated was deadly on her side and a shade perfunctory on his. Occasionally she betrays her stolidity of mind by a humourless suggestion, as when she begs him to make friends with her mother's crony, Joanna Baillie, since she is "of an age to prevent embarrassment." The advice reached him at Rotherham, where he was enjoying the company of his seventeen-year-old hostess, Frances Webster, a lovely young person born to create embarrassment. Did they laugh together over advice so ridiculously couched? Or were they too taken up with themselves to pay any attention to it?

Annabella's injunction that Lady Melbourne should be told nothing about their resumption of intercourse was not heeded by Byron. Writing from Rotherham he said, "the strictest of St. Ursula's 11,000 what-do-you-call-'ems has entered into a clandestine correspondence with a person generally esteemed a great roué."

An interchange of letters with so little life in them could not keep going long. By the end of October Byron reported to Lady Melbourne that it had died and that he would not resuscitate it. He counted without Miss Milbanke, who was determined not to let go. In November we find it resumed. She was frightfully dull at Seaham, and as the days shortened she began to mope and to study *The Giaour* in order to find out what

47

exactly Lord Byron had to say about "the tender passion."

> Yes, Love indeed is light from Heaven;
> A spark of that immortal fire
> With angels shared, by Allah given,
> To lift from earth our low desire
> Devotion wafts the mind above
> But Heaven itself descends in Love;
> A feeling from the Godhead caught,
> To wean from self each sordid thought;
> A ray of Him who formed the whole;
> A glory circling round the soul!

Such descriptions of love, she averred, "almost transported her" and made a poet's friendship seem more than ever desirable.

The family moved to Halnaby for the winter months. Early in November Annabella betrayed signs of huffiness; she desires to be informed whether her communications have become unacceptable, if so she will discontinue them. Byron was feverishly finishing *The Bride of Abydos* when he opened the letter, and this poem, whether written for Frances Webster or Augusta Leigh, was the outcome of emotions a great deal warmer than any Annabella could rouse in him. Realizing that he had offended her, he suggested a peace-offering of *The Bride*. In accepting it poor Miss Milbanke, who had a positive talent for standing in her own light, assured him that she has received "more pleasure from his poetry than from all the Q.E.D.s in Euclid." She studied his heroines, Leilas, Ginevras, Zuleikas, Medoras, all alike negative, lovely, and provocative of love.   Maybe she saw herself in the rôle of one of these houris.

> No danger daunts the pair his smile hath blest
> Their steps still roving, but their hearts at rest.
> With thee all toils are sweet, each clime hath charms
> Earth—sea alike—our world within our arms.

Politely and carefully the Childe answered her letters.   Pirouetting laboriously on paper, she made further efforts to capture his interest.   To meet him in London will be "one of the most agreeable incidents which my residence there can produce."   She has not been very well, she may not be up "to the labours of a London life."   It was all a little naïve, and Byron, who saw every situation in sharp outline, entered in his diary that the situation between himself and Miss Milbanke was an odd one "without a spark of love on either side."   Nothing vitalized their relation to each other; once more the correspondence languished.

As Christmas brought no letter, Annabella, on St. Stephen's Day, took up her pen to enquire what was happening to her friend.   Could Byron have gone abroad or had he merely lost interest in her again? Could there be anything wrong with her letters as they never seemed to produce the effect she intended? Lady Gosford perhaps could advise her on this point.

* * * * *

Byron had spent Christmas in London writing *The Corsair* at great speed, *con amore*, as he liked to phrase it.   Handing the poem over to John Murray, he waited to correct the proofs, then made his way to Newstead, where, in the "snow-bound, thaw-swamped valley of the shadow," he spent a cosy happy time with Goosey. Augusta Leigh had never visited Newstead before and was so delighted with the place that she begged him to desist from selling it as it was the very place to bring the children to in summer. Byron laughed, he was in excellent spirits: Goosey always amused him. He had other things to cheer him, for the success of *The Corsair* had been immediate. John Murray wrote that never, in his recollection, had any work created such a ferment. Ten thousand copies had been sold on the day of publication. This jubilation in success Goosey shared with the poet, while Annabella, dismally dull at Halnaby, was wandering about composing a poem on the recent fall of snow, a poem which in due course was posted to Byron. A letter reached him too, in which Miss Milbanke declared herself heart-free though doubtful of her suitability for married life. Though she is a free agent she questions her capacity for making another person happy, and this seems to suggest that his proposal of marriage should be renewed. Byron, it is clear, made this deduction; he replied by telling her that in London people were saying she had refused his suit a second time, an opening she was quick to seize, "as she has not been in a situation to refuse a second suit, she cannot consider herself as having refused it." A plain enough hint to which Byron riposted, "It would plague me much more to hear that I was accepted by anybody else than rejected by you."

Just exactly what could be read into this? To Annabella it seemed to indicate a willingness to persevere in friendship. To Byron it spelt capitulation, for to Lady Melbourne he wrote, "Your niece has committed herself perhaps."

*   *   *   *   *

In the spring of 1814 Lord Byron settled himself into Lord Althorp's vacated rooms in the Albany, took a box at the Opera, and accepted many invitations to dinners and routs. The poet was seen about a good deal with Tom Moore and Samuel Rogers. The season, which was particularly gay, was known as "the summer of the Sovreigns," for owing to the abdication of Napoleon Bonaparte, various royal personages were able to come to London to celebrate the end of a long and tedious war. Byron, when he heard that his poor little pagod Napoleon had been pushed off his pedestal, wrote the well-known lines:

> 'Tis done—but yesterday a King!
> And armed with Kings to strive—
> And now thou art a nameless thing:
> So abject—yet alive,

and entered in his diary, "a crown may not be worth dying for—yet to have outlived Lodi for this!"

It was the spring of Medora Leigh's birth, and many of Byron's spare thoughts were occupied by Gussy and her baby as his idler moments were spent playing with his new macaw. He was also busy during

51

May writing *Lara*, and on June 13 began his fair copy
of the poem.

*   *   *   *   *

Of all these activities and interests Miss Milbanke
in her northern exile knew nothing. An invitation
extended by her from Seaham had not been taken
advantage of and it almost seemed as if her friendship
with the Childe must slither to extinction. If writing
would save the situation, she would write and write in
terms that no one could possibly misunderstand. "I
should acknowledge without a blush that I have sought
your friendship." This sentence caught Byron's eye
in a letter opened at Hastings where he and Gussy were
staying with his friends Hodgson and George Lamb.
They were all celebrating the success of *Lara*. News
had just come that six thousand copies had been sold
in advance of publication. In the intervals of rejoicing
they diverted themselves by chaffing Byron about his
marriage. All agreed that it was time Byron took to
himself a wife. Gussy favoured a young friend of her
own and undertook to make an offer to her on her
brother's behalf.

This offer was made and in due course declined.
In the meantime Byron wrote to reassure Annabella
he "will always love her," he thinks that she would
"probably like him if she could." This seems to
mean very little, but it was all the encouragement Miss
Milbanke got.

At the end of August Gussy went to Newstead,

again taking with her the children, and in her company
Byron settled down to the only happy family life he was
ever to know. Gussy certainly understood him and
could make him laugh and relax as no one else could do.
With her he had no reserves: she read all his letters: she
discussed his future: she helped him to make preparations for his projected journey abroad. During September letters began to trickle in from Annabella, who
had taken up a new pose and now placed herself as a
pupil at Byron's feet. What should she read? Should
she try Gibbon, or would he like her to copy out for him
a passage from Porson? Here she was on ground that
Augusta could not occupy. Byron rose at once to the
Porson fly, wrote of Agricola and Suetonius, and then,
almost inconsequently and rather surprisingly, offered
himself in marriage to his correspondent in a letter
which Gussy laughingly declared to be so pretty that
it must be dispatched at once. Annabella, who had
at last triumphed, was surprised into a quick reply.
"This," she wrote, "is a moment of joy which I have too
much despaired of ever experiencing, I dare not believe
it possible." To make assurance doubly sure she
directed one letter of acceptance to Newstead and the
other to the Albany. They were not duplicates.

*　　*　　*　　*　　*

On the morning that Annabella's acceptance was
being discussed by Byron and Augusta at Newstead,
the gardener dug up from the flower-bed under what
had been Mrs. Byron's window a gold ring. It was

53

her wedding ring, and Byron and Gussy spoke of it as
"an omen." Some people, knowing that it had been
the symbol neither of fidelity nor happiness, might have
considered it an evil omen, but Byron solemnly declared
that he would wed his bride with it and none other.
Even light-hearted Gussy must have shrunk from so
insensitive a decision. With Annabella's letter by his
side Byron sat down to make known to his lawyer
Hanson that he had engaged himself to be married.
He stated that to the best of his belief Sir Ralph Milbanke must be deeply involved financially over his
electioneering. Miss Milbanke, however, must one
day become Baroness Noel and inherit property from
her uncle, Lord Wentworth. There will inevitably be
settlements made on her by her father and she will
inherit Seaham. So much for the business side of this
rather unromantic transaction.

A brisk interchange of letters, sometimes as many as
three in a day, now passed between the engaged couple.
It was very surprising to the parents at Seaham that the
spate of letters was not followed up by the writer.
Most inexplicably he tarried in the Albany. Sir Ralph
and Lady Milbanke had been ready to rejoice in the
engagement and broke the news of their daughter's
engagement to their relations in a series of suitable
missives. "It has taken place," wrote Lady Milbanke,
"with the entire approbation of her father and myself,
to which is added my brother's kindest sanction."
Annabella, writing in the same spirit, describes her
engagement as

an event that affords me the best prospect of happiness. The attachment had been progressive for two years and I now own it with feelings of happiness that promise to be durable as they are deep . . . for his despondency I fear I am but too answerable the last two years.

How flattering to self-esteem it was to write as if the most notable man in England had been languishing for her favour!

A formal announcement of the engagement was inserted in *The Morning Post* of October 5th, 1814. It provoked an avalanche of congratulatory letters, and Annabella's parents were for some weeks pleasantly occupied in replying to them and in making plans for the wedding. A wedding could not, however, be arranged altogether without consultation with a bridegroom, and where was the bridegroom? Why did he tarry? What was he doing? By what means could his conduct be explained? They fussed and worried to such an extent that Annabella, who was secretly disconcerted though she could not admit it, wrote to Byron, "The old ones are growing quite ungovernable . . . it is odd that my task should be to teach them patience."

It is noticeable that between September and Christmas Byron appears to have written no poetry. The fountain of his fancy no longer gushed in the old natural way, he seemed too distracted to settle down to writing. Douglas Kinnaird had suggested *Hebrew Melodies* to him as a theme, but he showed little interest in the project, and it was not till his marriage was over that he sat down to grind them out. The *Melodies* were intended to be set to music by Braham and Nathan, and were to be dedicated to the Princess Charlotte. From these and other indications we cannot doubt that Lord Byron was deeply perturbed at the idea of marrying, and his perturbance also manifested itself in shirking a visit to Seaham, the visit it had been expected he would pay the moment he had been accepted by Annabella. From the Milbankes' point of view his behaviour was offensive and inexplicable.

In this house of conventional illusions Annabella found herself awkwardly placed. She knew better than anyone that an engagement that brought no tokens of regard or demonstrations of devotion must seem, to say the least of it, a bald affair. No one would have welcomed the usual ring and presents more than she, but she could not for one moment admit it to her parents. She could dominate them only if she maintained her reserve, for they were still ready to accept all she said or did not say about her suitor, they were even ready to think that she lived and had her being in a more rarefied atmosphere than themselves, an atmosphere in which material manifestations of devotion were as dross. Though they recognized that they were people of ordinary feelings they did not find Annabella's aloof demeanour and pacifying words easy to understand. They had to take it on trust that it was the new fashion that a lover should not fly to his beloved, should not hasten to place a ring upon her finger, should not present himself to his family-to-be. It took all their good manners and self-control not to be constantly worrying their daughter with questions and complaints. When Lord Wentworth, Lady Milbanke's brother, proposed himself for a visit to meet his nephew-elect, it was extremely embarrassing to have no nephew for him to meet. For so very infirm a man to make a long journey, then a stay of three weeks and in the end to have to go south again having achieved nothing of what he set out to do was really mortifying. Annabella neither could nor would explain anything, but then as the weeks went by she was hard put to it to maintain her own equilibrium, much less restore that of anxious relatives.

Lord Byron was of course polite enough to make excuses for not proceeding to Seaham. He could not appear unaccompanied by his solicitor, and his solicitor was either ill or called to the country or very busy. Sir Ralph must be assured of his financial position; he would come when he could. It was not till some seven weeks after Annabella had accepted him as her future husband that Byron sent his solicitor ahead of him to Durham and left London himself to travel by slow stages to Seaham. Away from the Albany one Saturday morning in October sped a smart vis-à-vis with a moody looking young man sitting inside it. The first day's journey ended at Six-Mile Bottom—the home of Augusta Leigh. On the Monday he was still there and wrote to Lady Melbourne, "I am proceeding very slowly . . . I shall not stay above a week. . . . Don't write till you hear from me there. . . . I am not sure that I shall go now. . . . I am in very ill humour." After some kind of a scene with Gussy he posted north in a devilish temper. Damp cold weather combined with the depression of having pledged himself to marry a girl with whom he felt sure he was not in the least in love. It was enough to make anyone wretched.

The vis-à-vis drew up at last at the entrance to Seaham House and he was shown into the drawing-room on the first floor. It was empty. Annabella, who had been listening for the wheels of his chaise at the window in her schoolroom, walked through the drawing-room door. She saw Byron by the mantelpiece with his back to the fire; he did not move forward to greet her, but stood waiting to lift her outstretched hand to his lips. There was no thrill in the meeting, no spontaneity, no breaking down of barriers, it was a highly formal affair. In itself the immobility of the guest was nothing to go by, he made a habit of it as owing to his lameness he did not look his best in stepping forward; it always gave the effect of a run. As for Annabella, she might have been meeting a stranger. Here was she who during a whole year had thought of this man, planned to marry him, made a picture of him in her mind, now forced by the encounter to realize that the real man did not in any way correspond to the image she had made.

Byron was in as great a quandary. He recognized in a flash that her feeling for him was not instinctive and he told Lady Melbourne at once, "I have always thought her supposed *after-liking* for me was *imagination*." How could he bridge the gulf that seemed fixed between them? Could he awaken in her any feeling or was she fundamentally cold? Rather cynically he wrote to his confidante that he has had recourse to the eloquence of action . . . "to the calming process so renowned in our philosophy," but in this way he merely frightened the girl, who was inexperienced and timid. He was so odd she found when he worked himself up in this way, and she was apprehensive lest he should go too far. One day in a kind of paroxysm he fainted at her feet, which she took to be a proof of the strength of his love for her. As each day went by she found it more and more embarrassing to be alone in his company: how thankful she would be to be rid of him until the wedding day when, as she told herself, her feelings would be so miraculously transformed. Even Byron was obliged to admit "that being under the same roof and not married . . . well, past experience has shown us the awkwardness of the situation." Of one thing Miss Milbanke became increasingly sure, and that was that she must somehow get Byron out of the house: the strain of being with him was too great, he was too hard to understand, too familiar and too remote. Go he must until the time of the wedding had arrived. She therefore urged him to leave Seaham, though she did not at once make Lady Milbanke aware of her decision. The sooner he went, the sooner he would come back, and there was business enough to make an excuse for his departure valid. Byron felt the constraint though a little differently from Annabella; he was caught, "the die is cast; neither party can secede . . . I mean to behave attentively and well, though I could never love but that which loves," and Annabella had so far given no symptom of her capacity for doing this.

Preparations for the wedding went inexorably forward. Lawyers talked and settlements were drawn up. It had not taken Byron's solicitor long to discover that Miss Milbanke's prospects as an heiress were far from immediate. There was no ready money at all available, and twenty thousand pounds was the outside figure that could be raised on mortgage from Sir Ralph's already overcharged estate.

When the Milbankes began to discuss invitations, favours, presents, cake and clothes, they were cut short by the bridegroom, who said it was imperative that he should obtain a special licence from the Archbishop of Canterbury, so that they might dispense with banns and be married in any place and at any moment they liked. This proceeding seemed very odd to Sir Ralph and very disappointing to Lady Milbanke. Rather naturally they had planned to have county guests to the wedding and to entertain the tenantry and villagers. Over-ridden in this as in other matters by their high-handed son-in-law to be, they resignedly gave up their plans and conformed to his wishes. What else could they do? To cross him might provoke trouble and dear Nancy seemed to get more spiritless every day: she stood out for no rights and no conventions. When Byron had been at Seaham a fortnight he took his leave, and the parents were surprised to learn that their daughter had been responsible for shortening his stay. "The Elders," she wrote to her lover, "are not in very good humour with me as accessory to your departure."

When letters began to arrive from London again they contained annoying little bits of information conveyed flippantly, but, as Lady Milbanke grasped, full of purpose. "His godship Hymen has altogether given up white ribbon knots and the fooleries he used

to inflict upon his votaries. . . . I am told nobody has
them now—so don't let's be out of the fashion." In
this manner a further and as it turned out final blow was
dealt to the wedding plans of Lady Milbanke. No
favours? That meant presumably no bridesmaids, and
possibly, though it was almost unthinkable, no wedding
dress. Had ever bridegroom issued orders like these?

* * * * *

It is not easy to understand how Annabella kept her
will fixed on carrying the marriage through, for she was
sensitive in her own way and only too conscious of her
inability to charm her so-called lover. It is a little
pathetic to read how she tries to explain away their
innate incompatibility, "I certainly was not myself during your stay. . . . Myself is by no means the grave,
didactic, deplorable person that I have appeared to
you." She clung firmly to the belief that she was in
love with him and when taxed by Byron to tell him
whether she was quite sure that she loved him,
answered, "Why do you doubt it?" Buoying herself
up with the belief that marriage would make all the difference, she projected her mind forward into the hoped-
for bliss of wedlock and began to sign her letters
"Wife." Byron responded with "Sweetheart," "My
Love," and the rest. He, too, played at the game of
make-believe and, as a man without illusions, he certainly found it easier to be charming in absence than in
intercourse.

Left alone with her parents, Annabella found that all

conversation hovered round the wedding. Lady Milbanke thought it better that the ceremony should take place at Seaham rather than at Croft as Halnaby Hall would be such a comfortable place to go away to for the honeymoon. Sir Ralph kept harping on the theme of the bridegroom's quick return. So did his wife, but they kept their hopes and fears to themselves. For a night or two they went to Durham to see what their position would be after the proposed settlements had been signed. They were apprehensive lest they should have to part with Seaham, and it was a comfort when their solicitor told them that he did not think it obligatory. When the last days of November merged into December and the wintry light over the grey sea became more steely, the parents began to doubt whether they ought to have permitted their child's engagement to so eccentric a man. Not that they could really have prevented it, for Annabella, as they told each other, was headstrong and would never listen to their advice. From time to time scraps of news reached them. Lord Wentworth reported that he had called on his nephew-to-be in the Albany, adding a few polite remarks about the young man for his sister's benefit. Nancy occasionally let fall a word or two of information about her lover, and to their dismay at one moment seemed to be intending to go to London. They dared not ask why, but they were on tenterhooks about the possibility. Lady Melbourne, who had not approved of Byron's leaving Seaham, told him quite frankly that people were talking. He retorted that it was no fault of his. Every morning he received a letter from Annabella, "the snow is beginning to fall," "the wedding cake is a-making," "Papa is writing an Epithalamium." To each of them Byron replies, but sometimes with a wriggle, "To marry or not . . . that is the question . . . *or will you wait?* Perhaps the clouds will disperse in a month or two. Do as you please." She counters this Hamlet-like mood by pointing out that however little he and she may mind appearances, delays create vexation of spirit to her father and mother. "I am scolded everyday for your absence." "Are you less confident than you were in the happiness of our marriage?" and even, "Don't let me marry you against your will." The parents knew nothing of these vacillations and grew more and more despondent. Despondent, too, are the entries in Mr. Cam Hobhouse's diary. He had been booked for the part of best man, and it worried him to note the increased restlessness in Byron's manner. Tom Moore was depressed to hear that Byron considered himself entirely unfitted for married life. His friends were decidedly unhappy about him. On the eve of Christmas the bridegroom managed to screw himself up to the sticking point and set out once more alone for Newmarket. At Augusta's home he passed Christmas and from there wrote a letter to Annabella withdrawing from his engagement. Augusta, to whom he showed it, dissuaded him from sending it. He tore it up and composed another saying he was on his way north with a licence in his pocket. When Hobhouse joined him on the 26th of December he found him in a strange, indifferent mood, and almost averse to marriage. "Never was a lover less in haste."

The two men drove away from Augusta's house in perishingly cold weather. It was not till the evening of the 30th December that the watchers at Seaham heard a carriage draw up at the hall door. It was eight o'clock on a winter's night when handsome Mr. Hobhouse stepped out of the vis-à-vis, followed by his friend. Sir Ralph had given orders that his lordship and his friend were to be taken straight to their rooms, so there was no one to welcome them in the hall. After dressing for dinner Mr. Hobhouse went down to the library, where Sir Ralph, none too cordial, was waiting to greet him. Miss Milbanke came in to shake hands, but hearing an uneven footfall outside she rushed from the room and, throwing both arms round her bridegroom's neck, burst into tears.

On Mr. Hobhouse the bride made an impression of quiet dowdiness, there was something a little bit governessy about her as Tom Moore had noticed at Lady Cowper's party four years earlier, but then Mr. Hobhouse was fresh from London routs and Annabella had been living in the country for eighteen months, and none of her dresses was in the latest mode. Durham manty makers were always behind the times. He found her friendly, and was quite delighted to see that she watched Byron with what he interpreted as "adoring eyes."

The next day was taken up with signing settlements, some of which were contingent on the sale of Newstead. Sir Ralph had done his best, he had raised a twenty-thousand-pound mortgage and from its interest Byron would enjoy £700 a year and Annabella £300.

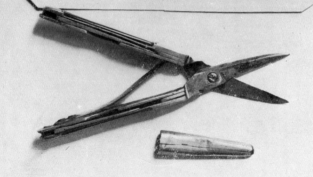

Thimble belonging to
Miss Elizabeth Pigot. It was
thrown three times into the
River Greet, and three times
the poet Lord Byron, dived,
and brought it up.

No other immediate prospect of income was anywhere discernible. For the time being the Byrons would be very poor, though both in time were likely to have money. Miss Milbanke must in the long run inherit property, and one day it might be possible to sell Newstead at a good price. If he had chosen, Byron could have made a small fortune by his poems, but this he scorned to do. To us his attitude about earning money appears fantastic, but it was consonant with the code of a gentleman of his day and one must remember that Walter Scott, a man of the professional classes, did not care for it to be known in the Law Courts that he wrote novels for a livelihood. How obstinately Byron clung to these conventions is proved by his refusing to accept a £1,500 cheque from John Murray when bailiffs were actually quartered in his Piccadilly home.

On the eve of New Year's Day, 1815, a half-comic rehearsal of the wedding ceremony took place in which Mr. Hobhouse took the part of the bride and Mr. Hoar, Sir Ralph's solicitor, the rôle of his employer. Next morning, the marriage day, was trying for everyone. Lady Milbanke was too nervous to pour out tea at breakfast, but Sir Ralph with his customary jocularity could be depended on to keep things going. Hobhouse came down fully dressed in wedding raiment with white gloves in his hands, but the bridegroom, less punctilious, wore his old coat and went out to prowl in the dene. He was certainly not going to don the hateful blue surtout till the last moment. Hobby had insisted on a new blue coat and blue was a colour he never fancied. Blue, Hobby had said, was the only wear at weddings, while he for his part had protested that either his bottle-green, his grey-green, or his olive-green surtout, all perfectly tailored, would do to be married in. Hobby had over-ruled him; green, he had said, was unlucky for weddings and blue he must wear.

The other breakfast guests were the Reverend Thomas Noel, an illegitimate son of Lord Wentworth, and Mr. Billy Hoar, the cheerful solicitor from Sunderland. When Mr. Wallace, the rector of Seaham, walked across the lawn from his house by the church, the party was complete.

The room that had been prepared for the wedding was the first-floor drawing-room, approached by a stairway from the front hall. As one enters this apartment one faces three bayed windows that overlook the garden behind the house. Few preparations had been made. Flowers were unobtainable. A table with service books occupied the bay; two hassocks were placed in the centre of the carpet, a few chairs against the walls; the clergymen stood with their backs to the cold daylight to await the arrival of the bride and bridegroom. The parents and Mr. Hoar stood on the left side of the room, and presently Lord Byron, who had been retrieved from the dene and arrayed in his blue surtout walked in with Mr. Hobhouse and took his place on the right by the fireplace. No one went to fetch the bride, but the gentlemen's entry was the signal for which Mrs. Clermont had been waiting to conduct her charge from the bedroom in which she had dressed to

66

the door of the drawing-room. Annabella entered alone. In a demure muslin gown, curricle jacket, and lace gloves, but without wreath or veil, she moved quietly to the left-hand hassock, where the bridegroom stood by her side. There, facing the windows with what composure they could muster, they went through the ceremony that was to unite them till death. In days when a stoical mien was expected and exacted on social occasions no allowances were made for "nerves," and such pandering to sensibility as allowing the principal parties to stand with their backs to the light it would have occurred to no one of that date to engineer.

Fortunately for all concerned the service was short and the hassocks on which the couple had to kneel hard enough to claim attention. When at the clergyman's bidding Lord Byron produced a ring and slipped it over the bride's finger, it was noticed that the ring did not fit, it looked as if made for another person. And so it had been, for it was the heavy gold ring dug up from the flower-bed at Newstead that now hung on the girl's finger. The usual vows were exchanged and "man and wife together" were blessed in well-worn phrases. Rising from her knees Annabella submitted to the kisses of her parents and then slipped half-tearful from the room. In a few moments she was back in apparent control of her emotions and ready to proceed downstairs on Byron's arm to cut the towering wedding cake. After health-drinking and felicitations were over, Mrs. Clermont reminded her charge that she must change quickly into her travelling dress, a dove-coloured pelisse of soft satin.   There was reason for haste, it would be dark at four o'clock and the newly wed couple had forty miles to drive.

Before Lady Byron had emerged from her room, Lord Byron's carriage drew up at the front door. Annabella soon appeared, made scurried farewells and was about to mount into the vehicle assisted by the best man when she was startled by the firing of muskets and the pealing of church bells.   When she had seated herself, Hobby gripped his friend's hand, feeling, as he afterwards said, as if he was "burying him."   At the last moment he pushed his wedding present to Lady Byron into the seat beside her, a set of her husband's works bound in yellow morocco.   Parents, best man, guests, all stood with fixed smiles on the doorstep till the coachman touched the horses with his whip and the carriage rolled forward past the wind-clipped sycamores on to the Durham road.

Hardly was the strain of the actual ceremony over than the wear and tear of life together made itself felt. Unlike other lovers the world over this couple found no solace in mutual solitude.   Perhaps it was the weather that made Byron so irritable.   He had always hated snow and now he was being forced to drive for hours on wintry roads to a destiny that he could not face with any equanimity.   Temperamentally a southerner and a sun-worshipper, he never, save by his accent, seemed to be identified with Scotland, the land in which he had been reared.   At Newstead on snowy days he had stayed in bed and kept the curtains drawn so as not to have to look out on the whitened lawns.   The prospect of a honeymoon in the uncongenial climate of northern England in the uncongenial month of January was almost insupportable. The wedding had been bleak enough, the sequel began even more bleakly. Making no effort to disguise his displeasure or his irritability, he vented his feelings on the only person within reach, who also happened to be the immediate cause of his condition.

The vis-à-vis trotted along the Durham road with both occupants acutely conscious of want of ease in the other's company. Byron at first was silent, then sang snatches of what Annabella thought must be Albanian songs. What could she do to placate or divert him? As she looked from the carriage windows the view was not inspiring—undulating fields powdered with snow, and hedges and trees showing black against the blanched landscape. While they halted at a livery stable in Durham it began to snow and through the snow they heard the pealing of cathedral bells. "Ringing for our happiness?" cynically queried the bridegroom. Once more on the road he gave utterance to his ravaging thoughts. His marriage had come too late to save him; he belonged to Augusta till death and beyond. "It must come to a separation," he muttered. "You should have married me when I first proposed." Frightened and half in tears, Annabella braced herself up by assuming that her husband was indulging in some horrible form of fun. She murmured a few pacifying words only to be countered with "I will be even with you yet," but catching sight of her scared expression he relented and spoke kindly to her. Up till the halt in

Durham Annabella's old maid had been sitting outside
in the rumble. Now owing to the heavy fall of snow
she was told by her mistress to sit inside on the back
seat. It annoyed Byron extremely to have a maid and
bandbox in contact with his knee. The next halt was
at the inn by Rushyford cross-roads. The local legend
is that they got out there and had a glass of porto; one
is even shown the room in which they sat. Rushyford
cross-roads is now a dangerous corner for motorists, but
on that winter's night there were no other passengers
on the road or at the inn. Annabella records that
during the wait Byron remarked that he was discon-
tented with the settlements and spoke to her "as if I
were a beggar." He also wondered how long he would
be able to play the part allotted to him. A less-con-
soling companion for a journey it would have been
impossible to find.

The road from Rushyford to Darlington was straight,
but they could see nothing as they peered out of the
fogged windows till they came to the lights of North
Gate. Rattling over the market-place setts the chaise
took the Croft road. There were still five miles to go
and every step of the way had been familiar to Annabella since childhood. Never had she travelled it in
such despondency. At Croft bridge they crossed the
Tees to the Yorkshire bank. The horses were whipped
up through the village, past the Spa, on to the Middleton Tyas lane and then turned in at Halnaby Hall
gates, which were opened by a bowing pair of Milbanke
employees. It was pitch dark in the drive, but the
housekeeper, Mrs. Minns, having left the ground-floor

windows unshuttered, the light of yellow candles shone out into the night.

Stiff with long sitting, Lord and Lady Byron walked up the steps to the door unsmiling and entered the house. The servants afterwards said that they expected the newly wed couple to be arm-in-arm and even laughing, but they walked in independently and dejectedly. Though the principals were not playing the part expected of them the retainers were determined to play theirs. Mrs. Minns curtseyed to her ladyship and the butler made a little speech of welcome. His lordship's valet, Fletcher, who had gone ahead with the luggage, helped his master off with his redingote, disclosing as he did so, the hated blue livery donned for the wedding ceremony.

Byron looked round the large hall in which he found himself. It was floored with marble and its walls were decorated with stucco festoons in the Italian taste. It was very different from his own denuded home from which all the ornament had been torn down by his mad grandfather. Presently Mrs. Minns led the way upstairs to the first-floor corridor on which the bedrooms were situated. Opening the door of two rooms communicating with each other by means of a paper-covered door, she stood aside to let the couple pass. Fires were burning brightly and Byron noticed that "her ladyship's room" contained a bed with red moreen curtains. The rooms allotted to them were none too commodious and they faced the north. Mrs. Minns, either by order or of her own initiative, had made ready the second-best bedrooms, the larger ones were on the south side of the house.

Changing their crumpled clothes they went down to dine in a comfortable parlour off the hall. Byron had been a little mollified by inspecting the library, which looked snug and faced south, and it is probable that with the assistance of good Milbanke claret and old port they got through the evening creditably so far as the servants were concerned. After dinner when they were alone Byron asked his wife with every appearance of aversion whether she meant to sleep in the same bed with him, adding, "I hate sleeping with any woman, but you may if you choose," following this up with a cruel touch, "provided a woman was young, one was as good as another."

At night they enclosed themselves within the red curtains of a small four-post bed. The firelight flickered through the material, making a red glow, and Byron woke up from his first sleep with a start to give utterance to the famous exclamation, "Good God! I am surely in Hell!" Annabella spoke later on of his alarming habits and the way he prowled up and down the corridor at night armed with pistol and sword. It may have been these strange nocturnal fears that caused Annabella to entreat him (if Countess Guiccioli is to be believed) at this time to give up versifying, and when she left him for the last time in Piccadilly a year later she also begged him to give up versifying *and* brandy. The writing of poetry was evidently associated in her mind with terrifying mental excitement.

To men who hunted and fished and shot and talked

endlessly about these sports Annabella was well accustomed.   In the world she had left, men got up for a solid breakfast, spent the day out of doors and sat up after dinner to drink port or play faro.   At night or in the small hours they lay down beside their wives in dreamless slumber.   A husband of this sort would have been no problem to Annabella, but here she was shut up alone with a person who, judged by her father's standards, was more like a foreign nobleman than an English gentleman, a man who pursued no sport, who never ate breakfast and never played cards, and above all was subject to the most unaccountable changes in mood.

When Byron looked out of the window on the morning after the arrival at Halnaby he saw a white expanse of ground and a pond covered with ice.   It was the kind of outlook that made him shudder and return to the comfort of his curtained bed.   No longer as at Newstead his own master, he felt obliged on this particular morning to get up.   Joining Annabella downstairs about midday, he was shown the inside and the outside of his father-in-law's handsome red-brick house. Built under the Commonwealth and crowned by balustrading, it stood foursquare to a park peopled with deer, foxes, and hares.   It was a fine solid place and a nice property, but of little interest to Lord Byron as, being entailed on a male cousin, it could never come to Annabella.

On this first honeymoon morning the bridegroom was handed a letter from Augusta Leigh, in which, addressing him as "Dearest, first and best of human

73

beings," she described the emotion that had overcome her at the hour of his marriage, it was "as the trembling of the sea when the earth quakes." So untimely a reminder of their common sensibility and of the fundamental oneness of their relationship was under the circumstances unforgivable. Gussy's conduct at this crisis inclines one to agree with Lady Melbourne, who called her "a clever, wicked woman," rather than with those persons who summed her up as a moral idiot. She may, however, have been both. In Byron the letter stirred up the memory of happier, freer days, and made him chafe against his present condition. He mumbled to Annabella that he was a villain to have married her and that of course their union must be accursed. Annabella, who was floundering in her efforts to interpret his moods, asked him one day to tell her something about the play *Don Sebastian* by Dryden. He at once became angry, excited and disagreeable, for the theme of the play was incest. His wife dropped the subject. Both of them spent most of their time in the library: Byron became engrossed with the Journal of the regicide Ludlow, whose exile at the Lake of Geneva had been mitigated by the faithful companionship of his wife, while Annabella walked about picking books at random from the shelves. Few honeymoons can have been less amusing or more wholly secluded.

By favour of John Murray, Byron received a special mail-coach copy of *The Lord of the Isles*. This they read aloud to each other by turns. Annabella volunteered to make a fair transcription of *Hebrew Melodies* which Byron was at the time endeavouring to compose.

By the Rivers of Babylon and *Herod's Lament* were both
written at Halnaby.   From time to time as she worked
for him they had to laugh; after all they were very
young to be in a perpetual state of gloom, but on the
whole Byron was in low spirits and would often refuse
to be roused.   Even the best days had their depressed
hours; it was all very unlike his honeymoons with
Goosey.   So acutely did Annabella feel the inadequacy
of her company and the constraint of being alone with
her husband that she took the extraordinary step of
inviting Augusta Leigh, whom she now alluded to as
"our sister," to join them at Halnaby.   She had told
Byron at Seaham that there was no one with whom she
would sooner share his society than Mrs. Leigh, but it
is difficult to believe that this was really true.   Gussy,
at any rate, had the common decency to refuse the
strange invitation "to participate" in what Byron called
the "treaclemoon."   It droned uninterruptedly on.

On Sundays they went to the village church and
made what must have been a sensational appearance as
they climbed the wide stairway to the Halnaby pew.
Once inside the box no one could see what they did, but
entry and exit were scrutinized by every eye.   And was
it any wonder that the villagers stared their fill at the
smartly-attired young man with the pale beautiful face
who had married their young lady from the Hall?
What sort of a husband would he make for their rosy-
cheeked Miss Nancy, who had grown so wisely from
babyhood to girlhood as the apple of her parents' eyes?
The bridegroom had, by all accounts, a country seat of
his own, and the vicar had said he was a poet like Walter

75

Scott and nearly as well liked, but poetry was hardly a profession for a gentleman, while for a lord it must be merely a pastime. Perhaps he went in for politics, perhaps he made grand speeches in the House of Lords. If the servants were to be believed, the honeymoon was a queer business. Lord Byron, it seemed, never went out of doors. It was said that he sat over the library fire scribbling or reading all day long and half the night. What a way for a newly married man to behave!

After twenty days of seclusion at Halnaby the vis-à-vis once more took the road. The Byrons returned to Seaham and for nearly seven weeks domiciled themselves with the Milbankes. Lady Milbanke, determined to make the best of things, told her brother-in-law, Sir James Burgess, that "the newly wedded couple seemed as happy as youth and love can make them." It was her considered opinion that "Lord Byron preferred a quiet domestic circle to any other and that neither of them were in any haste to get to London."

Truth to tell, the relief of not being shut up alone together was enormous. Byron became quite cheerful and joked with his mother-in-law, who was easier company than his wife. He even allowed himself to be taken along the shore to the Feather-bed Rocks and back, and owing to Annabella's rosy cheeks, made so much more rosy by the seawinds, would call her Pippin-pip-pip, the cry of the apple-sellers in London. As for his wife, she began to lose her fear of Byron and almost to enjoy his company. It seemed as though the marriage might turn into a success after all. The reaction, however, did not long endure and soon Byron began to write letters to Tom Moore saying that he is in such a state of "sameness and stagnation" that he has no sense left. He describes life at Seaham as a yawning over newspapers, *Annual Registers* and dull games of cards. For exercise he gathers shells upon the seashore and watches the growth of stunted gooseberries in the kitchen garden. Dismal and restricted as he found life to be, it was not made more bearable by Augusta, whose letters undid such good as the sea air and rest might be doing to his health. He always repined, for he felt trapped, though he found it easier to write at Seaham than at Halnaby. These lines were written at Seaham:

> Oh could I feel as I have felt—or
>   be what I have been
> Or weep as I could once have wept, o'er
>   many a vanished scene
> As springs in deserts found are sweet,
>   all brackish though they be
> So, midst the wither'd waste of life,
>   those tears would flow to me.

And so were a number of the *Hebrew Melodies*, *Saul*, *Song of Saul before his last battle*, *All is Vanity*, *When Coldness wraps this suffering Clay*, and then the best known of all the *Melodies*, *The Destruction of Sennacherib*:

> The Assyrian came down like the wolf on the fold,
> And his cohorts were gleaming with purple and gold;
> And the sheen of their spears was like stars on the sea
> Where the blue wave rolls nightly on deep Galilee.

77

Like the leaves of the forest when Summer is green,
That host with their banners at sunset were seen:
Like the leaves of the forest when Autumn hath blown,
That host on the morrow lay withered and strown.

Goaded after a while to frenzy by his longing for
Augusta's company, there came a day when the Milbankes could no longer hold him.   To Gussy he must
go.   Annabella from a mixture of motives, her right as
a wife, her curiosity to see Augusta at home, her fear of
losing ground with Byron, made up her mind to travel
with him to Newmarket.   Byron entreated her not to
come, but she refused to be persuaded to any other
course, with the result that under Augusta's roof she
learnt beyond all reasonable doubt the secret of her
husband's desperate moods.   With the piety in which
she sometimes took refuge, Augusta reported to a
friend that Byron's nerves and spirits during the visit to
Newmarket were very far from what she could wish but
that "the Almighty she trusts will be graciously pleased
to grant him those inward feelings of peace and calm
which are now so unfortunately wanting."

The fate of Byron and his bride is still a living issue
that people debate and interpret according to their
lights or their prejudices.   No one who has tried to
render the story from the Seaham angle can fail to be
utterly convinced of the incongruity of the match.
Matrimony after this sort could end in nothing but the
dislocation of two lives.   Could Annabella and her
husband revisit Seaham they would find the sheltered
dene and the strand unaltered.   For the rest they would

fly disconsolate from the changed scene of their irreparable mistake.

*　　*　　*　　*　　*

I have been in and out of Halnaby Hall at different times of the year.　The front door no longer opens into the Italianate hall for the entrance is now on the south side of the house.　By the present owner I have been shown the famous bedroom and to my enquiry whether the red curtains that draped the bed were the honeymoon hangings, was told that they were not.　All that was left of that material covered two chairs on the staircase.　A drawer full of odds and ends was opened in the hall and to my great pleasure I was given a piece of the original moreen that had been cut off when the chair coverings were shaped.　Of this trophy I feel as proud as does Sir John Murray of a similar fragment that he has framed in his editorial room at 50 Albemarle Street.　Yet another link was forthcoming, a set of verses that the present owner of Halnaby found many years ago jammed at the back of a drawer in a writing-table.　It is a fair copy in Lady Byron's handwriting of the poem beginning:

> Without a stone to mark the spot,
> And say, what Truth might well have said,
> By all, save one, her name forgot,
> Ah! wherefore art thou lowly laid?
> By many a shore and many a sea
> Divided, yet beloved in vain.

79

These lines *To Thyrza* had been written in 1811 and published in *Childe Harold* in 1812. The identity of Thyrza was said to be a mystery; Augusta Leigh may have known who she was as she had a manuscript copy of the poem in Byron's handwriting. Lady Byron recorded years later that she had once been shown by her husband "a beautiful tress of hair . . ." which she "understood to be Thyrza's." The poem ends with a plea:

> But if in worlds more blest than this
> Thy virtues seek a fitter sphere,
> Impart some portion of thy bliss,
> To wean me from mine anguish here.
> Teach me—too early taught by thee!
> To bear, forgiving and forgiven:
> On earth thy love was such to me;
> It fain would form my hope in Heaven.

I like to think that this scrap of paper is a relic of the honeymoon, as there seems little doubt that it must be. After several visits to Halnaby and re-reading the Byron letters I went to sit on the steps of the opera-box pew in Croft church to think over the subjects of my story. As I walked away through the graveyard an educated voice said to me, "Are you aware that Lewis Carroll lived in Croft rectory as a boy?" It was that of the rector, who kindly showed me round the garden in which the author of *Alice in Wonderland* had once played.

WORDSWORTH AT SOCKBURN

F

WORDSWORTH AT SOCKBURN

Ewig jung ist nur die Phantasie
Was sich nie und nirgends hat begeben
Das allein veraltet nie.

SCHILLER

Our temporary home in Durham was a Victorian house by a deep sliding section of the river Tees. Edged with alders, thornbrakes, and coarse grass it was as unlike the visionary Teesdale of childish recollection with its gentians, primulas, and jumping trout as anything that is essentially the same could be. Winds from the east brought with them factory fumes and sometimes a menacing pall that dimmed the sky: the river soon imposed itself on me as a symbol of human life with its eager bright beginning and its sluggish unlovely ending. Prolonged and crippling illness inclines one to morbidity and during the first winter that I tottered up and down the short beat of the Tees adjacent to our house I felt that no English landscape could be less sympathetic. There was a moment in spring when the shorn woods on the other shore became starred with primroses and another lovely moment when a family of kingfishers flashed in and out of a hole in a sandy bluff and reminded me of the kingfishers that had comforted Wordsworth in his icy tramps at Goslar. Against these comforts I balanced the flounder, the eels, the chub, and the occasional small dark trout that persistent family fishing brought to my bedside. The Tees was not so unlike the repellent Ouse

with its suicides' backwater above York and its slow
stream drifting through the Ings below.   Not till I
regained personal mobility and freedom from swinging
temperatures was it possible for me to take a less-
jaundiced view of my immediate surroundings.   Once
I could go where I would, however, things began to
happen, surprises that put all miseries to flight and
replaced them with happiness and lightness of heart.
The drifting river unmasked to reveal a magical and
contortionist vitality.   Down-stream I found that it had
bored for itself a convoluted channel water sometimes
flat and sometimes cliff-like configuration of bank which
in combination with the quickened tempo of the current
produced an effect startling in contrast to the straight
stream I had watched week in week out from my bowed
bedroom window.   Particularly in the reaches above
the ancient weir, Fishlocks, did I discover that the Tees
had scooped out deep loops of pasture and woodland in
which farms and homesteads lay in eighteenth-century
seclusion, a seclusion I would not have believed it
possible to preserve in the neighbourhood of an industrial town had I not seen it with my own eyes.   The
scene was

> As safe and sacred from the step of man
> As an invisible world—unheard, unseen.

If the sinuous strange character of the river surprised
me, it surprised me still more to find that these very
reaches had once been loved by a poet.   When in reading the early letters of William and Dorothy Wordsworth I learnt that William Wordsworth had paced

these pastures, meditated in these woods, made poetry in this place, the country lost its insignificance and became for me invested with the distilled radiance which the mind of a poet alone can impart. Here then amid the long silences of Durham woods and fields had the greatest of our lyric poets found a retreat so squaring with his desire as to win from it the deep happiness of inner receptivity. I owe much to Wordsworth, even more to Coleridge, and it sometimes seems to me that if there had been no poets to bestow their souls on our souls, our lives would be deprived of half their sense and much of their meaning, for is not the mission of the poet to save us from disintegration? In order to write poetry at all a man must be equipped with a steely conviction of his own identity:

> Adventure most unto itself
> The Soul condemned to be;
> Attended by a Single Hound
> Its own Identity.

To Keats the uplands of Hampstead had once afforded the solitude necessary to creation and poets once walked among the bluebells and Solomon's seal in what Dickens liked to call "the forest of San Giovanni." Though the poets are dead, these wildflowers push their way up faithfully each spring in the garden plots of the Victorian villas that have long since replaced the groves. Men may have failed, the flowers at least keep tryst. It is because the peninsula of Sockburn now stands to the fast-expanding industrial town of Darlington in the same relation as the Wood of St. John once stood to

London that I explored this loop of verdure with something like apprehension at heart.

*　　*　　*　　*　　*

Once partitioned between two families of ancient gentry—that of Conyers and that of men so proud of their riverside estates as to call themselves super-Teysam or sur-Tees, the Sockburn area is steeped in English history. In reading the *Itinerary* of Leland I found that he, having visited the place in the reign of Henry VIII, had recorded his interview with the Conyers then in possession of "the mile cumpass of exceeding pleasant ground that almost made an isle as Tese River windedeth about it." The "tumbe of Sir John Coniers," the "great were for fisch," "the umbrageous trees," were all pointed out to this visitor, who made a special note of the short turf "sacred from the plough" before starting to ride to "Niseham-on-Tees" and trot through "pure good corne" to "Daryngton." But this was in the sixteenth century, and when the antiquarian, Robert Surtees, inventoried the place some three hundred years later there was little trace of former occupation. He described the church by the ford "standing lonely on its level green, surviving the halls of its patrons the Conyers," he noted to the south of the church the mound where once the castle had stood, and deep traces of foundations and gardens, but of the planting nothing survived but "a decaying Spanish chestnut." His record takes on the tinge of melancholy as he pictures "the long lineal procession of

86

gallant knights and esquires" who held Sockburn
Castle till the Civil War that dispossessed so many old
families of their estates. "All are fallen," he wrote,
"not a foot of land is held by a Conyers, and of their
house not one stone is left upon another." Sitting by
the river ford balancing Surtees's great volume on my
knees, my eye traversed the many ancient scars now
veiled by velvet herbage, and inevitably the lines of
John Clare suggested themselves as caption to the
scene:

> And still the grass eternal springs
> Where castles stood and grandeur died.

*   *   *   *   *

It was to this rustic unremembered place that
William and Dorothy Wordsworth came straight from
Germany to stay with their Penrith kinsfolk, the Hutchinsons, to whom the farm had fallen by inheritance.
It had long been in Dorothy's mind to introduce
William to its delights discovered by her two years
earlier. She had even suggested, when the further
tenancy of Alfoxden had been denied them, that they
should go to Durham rather than venture abroad.
William had declined to do so as Coleridge and his
adoring friend, John Chester, were about to go to
Hamburg and had pressed the Wordsworths to come
too, with the result that the four of them set sail from
Yarmouth for the Continent on September 16th, 1798.
At Hamburg they talked with the poet, Klopstock, still
wearing a powdered tye-wig with a high toupée of hair

sloping back from the forehead. It touched some string in Dorothy's heart to hear that this puckered dropsical old gentleman with his lively French manners had once planted a yew tree on the grave of his first wife in Altona. She noted with pride that William's French made him an easier conversationalist than Coleridge, whose few German phrases did not serve to express his thoughts. At Hamburg the quartet rather unexpectedly split up, William and Dorothy going to the sombre city of Goslar and the others to Ratzeburg.

During the winter at Goslar, the coldest within memory, William and Dorothy bought furs that defied the arctic air. True to his love for nocturnal rambles, William walked about by moonlight in his gown and black fur cap, looking as Dorothy said for all the world like "a grand Signior." Constrained to take his mind off the glacial misery of their lodgings by composition, Wordsworth wrote many poems, but neither he nor his sister learnt much German or got on with German folk. Towards the end of February they walked away through the Harz forests towards Nordhausen and arrived in Göttingen in April. There they found Coleridge absorbed in work and "quite inappreciative of English conversation." The friends had not kept pace with each other linguistically: Coleridge, they were surprised to find, could discuss anything in German, whereas they had picked up but a few sentences. He seemed happy and they had been unhappy. All that one writer wanted was to be left at peace in Germany, and all that the other wanted was to go home to England. A little cast down by Coleridge's obvious wish to be quit of them, brother and sister made their way to Cuxhaven, embarked for Yarmouth, and thence drove to Durham.

At Entercommon on the Northallerton-Darlington road they dismounted from the stage-coach to find George and Thomas Hutchinson awaiting them. Dorothy, short, slight, with startled brown eyes, rushed forward with a stammered greeting, her tanned face beaming with pleasure. Coleridge when he first knew her said she was "a woman indeed, with manners simple, ardent, and impressive," but De Quincey found her "unsexual looking" and awkward in movement. Even he, however, had to admit that anyone to whom "the temple of her fervent heart had been thrown open" ceased to cavil at her ways or comment on her appearance. Behind Dorothy advanced tall William, not yet thirty, but with head reflectively bent and manner so austere as to present a staid counterweight to his over-eager sister.

Dorothy's personal luggage was as usual exiguous, and such books and bundles as the pair brought with them could easily be carried from stage-halt to ford. The Hutchinson brothers led their horses down to the river and then transported their guests pillionwise from the Yorkshire to the Durham bank of the Tees. Four dogs barked in chorus on the far bank, two greyhounds, Dart and Swallow, and two beagles, Prince and Music. Wordsworth, with whom one does not associate love of dogs, took a fancy to the little pack and even wrote verses in their praise. The farmhouse they were approaching stood some four hundred yards away on a slight elevation, presiding, as they saw it, over a green loop of pasture, "nearly washed round," as Dorothy observed, "by flowing water." Built in the eighteenth century by an uncle of the Hutchinsons, the structure, though not without architectural grace, is to local memory without associations. Always had Dorothy impressed on William that the farm was not at all like a farm to look at, and Robert Surtees, who never cared about modern buildings, said that it was "something better and worse than a farm." I could see for myself when I went to photograph the place how right they were, for the brick house with its two wings, tall chimneys, fan-lighted door and formal apron-garden still looks elegant, though it has always been in working occupation.

The welcome given to the travellers by Mary Hutchinson and her round-about little sister, Sara, was warm. Blue-eyed and fair and, in spite of a squint, benign in expression, Mary aged thirty, a year older than William and two years older than Dorothy, was the pillar of the household. Though friendly of mien Mary was tongue-tied and so silent that Thomas Clarkson used to say the only words that came easily from her lips were "God bless you!" Sara, though plain, was far more intelligent and ventured at times to discuss and even to criticize William's poems as well as to write verse herself. The brothers, as Southey tells us, were illiterate, worthy men and good farmers.

To Dorothy's delight her brother took at once to the place and the company. It has been suggested that as a boy at a Dame's school in Penrith William had fallen in love with Mary, but even if this were true much had

THE HOME FARM, SOCKBURN

happened since those days and it was not as lovers that they now met. Exile in Germany had taught Wordsworth, as he owned to Joseph Cottle, "to know the value of England." He was "right glad" to find himself among the fields and woods of his own country. Indeed, the contrast between the windswept ramparts of Goslar and the soft spring paradise of Sockburn lapped him in content. It had been a surprise to Dorothy on her first visit to the Hutchinsons to find rural life going so smoothly. It still went smoothly and none of the afflictions she associated with farm work seemed to worry her hosts. There was no early morning scramble to get up in the dark, and no importation of mud by hobnailed boots. Owing to Mary's quiet industry daily duties were unobtrusively performed, and as for the outdoor work, apart from the flocks of sheep, there were but two cows and some chickens to be cared for. The young Hutchinsons, like their forerunners, used their virgin fields in the traditional manner for grazing and just as in Leland's day cultivated but a very small acreage of cornland. Among neighbouring farmers the pasture had always been famed for flocks of fat short-horned sheep, and at Darlington one may see an account in the local register of a prize shorthorn from Sockburn. It had been shown by the Hutchinsons' uncle with five inches of fat on its rump and a shoulder that when salted weighed twenty-five pounds!

From the raised apron-garden Dorothy watched the lambs frisking, and primly says these gambolling creatures gave the estate "a very interesting appearance."

Beyond the pasture she could see a cornfield with a stone protruding from the soil, a kind of submerged rock about which ploughmen, as Mary told her, had for centuries drawn concentric furrows. This limestone lump was reputed to mark the grave of the great Wyvern slain by a Conyers some thousand years earlier. The falchion with which he despatched the monster was held as a title to the lands of the peninsula and even now serves as an instrument of conveyance. A local resident told me that within her memory an effort had been made to blow up the rock. This had cracked its surface but had in no wise improved the cornfield. Who knew what ill-luck might ensue if an object respected through the centuries were disturbed, things of the sort were best let be.

Away to the left as I looked out from the apron-garden where the ground sloped to the ford stood the little parish church where lay "the arméd" knight. It was to this place that the Hutchinsons repaired on Sundays and in this graveyard their forebears lay buried. Still closer to the ford I could discern the mounds of the old fortalice that once had kept ward by the river.

Day after day William and Dorothy explored the countryside. They were both great walkers, but they never seem to have wandered into Darlington, at that time a Quaker city of severely Puritan behaviour wherein rebellious little William Bewick was growing up and wherefrom he fled to the freedom of the Royal Academy Schools. Towns the Wordsworths always avoided unless business obliged them to be there. Cut off from Yorkshire by the Tees, they stayed on the Durham bank of the river and drew excitement from "every flower that feeds itself on British air in wilding pomp." The rare intensity of Dorothy's perceptions acted, it would seem, as a lightning conductor on the soul of her companion. Tuning in to the changing seasons, she outpoured her essential music on the only human being she was ever completely to understand and adore, her brother William.

Nothing in nature escaped the Wordsworths' interest. At Fishlocks they watched the salmon leaping by the weir, listened to the cry of the peewit, glanced at the sweeping pinion of the heron, considered "lychnis, willow-herb, fox-glove bells" and even "the tuft of wingéd seed mounted on a dandelion's naked stalk." And as Coleridge says they looked into the river where each

> . . . pool became a mirror; and behold
> Each wildflower on the marge inverted there.

As I wandered by the long walls of Fishlocks' manor garden exulting in the pear-blossom that gleamed from their ruddy expanse and, pushing on through undergrowth, came on hot springs in which Roman legionaries had bathed and on oxlips in the spinney that shrouded them, I realized the Wordsworths must have done these very things too. Up-stream they must have walked beside the warm and sparkling shallows to Hurworth Green and, stepping along the slender Roman road, hung over the great stone bridge at Croft. We know that they met no one on their rambles save perhaps in a village street, a state of affairs so entirely to

93

their taste that they were beguiled to spend more than eight months at Sockburn watching spring turn into summer, summer slide into autumn and autumn become winter. Having myself walked the banks at all seasons of the year, I can say they are almost as undisturbed now as they were a century and more ago. "The universal hours" may still be reckoned there by "succeeding tribes of animals or plants, joy on joy, plenitude on plenitude." For a poet seeking to respond to a celestial call Sockburn was the ideal refuge.

I was naturally curious as to what poems were written in this retreat. The boredom and acute discomfort experienced in Germany I knew had galled Wordsworth into producing a great deal of verse and that in the January following their arrival at Goslar Dorothy had been able to forward to Coleridge "some poems out of the mass" William had written. The first book of *The Prelude* was at this time submitted to their friend, and so probably were *Lucy Gray, Ruth* and some of *The Poems founded on the Affections*. Whether the "Lucy" lyrics composed during Dorothy's sickness at Goslar were really animated by William's devotion to Dorothy, no one now can with certainty say, but Coleridge, who understood the relation of William to Dorothy better than any other person, always believed that *A Slumber did my Spirit steal* was inspired by the thought of his sister's death, and yet another lyric, *Strange Fits of Passion I have known*, by the panic in absence lest "Lucy" should be dead. The second of *The Poems founded on the Affections*, the poem that discloses William's relief at finding himself in England

94

again, was certainly, as Professor de Selincourt admits, written by the banks of Tees.

> I travelled among unknown men
>   In lands beyond the sea
> Nor, England! did I know till then
>   What love I bore to thee.
>
> 'Tis past, that melancholy dream!
>   Nor will I quit thy shore
> A second time; for still I seem
>   To love thee more and more.
>
> Among thy mountains did I feel
>   The joy of my desire;
> And she I cherished turned her wheel
>   Beside an English fire.
>
> Thy mornings showed, thy nights concealed
>   The bowers where Lucy played;
> And thine too is the last green field
>   That Lucy's eyes surveyed.

And there can be little doubt that *The Poet's Epitaph*, if not entirely composed at Sockburn, at least received its present form there. But actual performance apart, there was a continual garnering of the material for future poems and unceasing work on *The Prelude*.

* * * * *

Almost unobservedly the happy meads of Sockburn became the scene of Wordsworth's courtship of his hostess, but it was an approach so cool and so deliberate as to be unrecognized as a wooing till Coleridge, bursting in on the family party after its six months' estrangement from the world, saw in a flash that his friend William had fallen in love with Mary Hutchinson, patient silent Mary who was devoting hour after hour to copying *The Borderers* from William's revised manuscript.   It was no light thing to be the wife, daughter, sister or friend of a poet, for to save the family genius from drudgery they might be called on to make fair copies of half-illegible script.   Even Lady Byron was set to transcribe poems during the honeymoon at Halnaby as well as in the more turbulent days in Piccadilly.   William had come to depend on Mary for service of this kind, with the natural result that companionship developed into understanding and eventuated into a tacit albeit undeclared devotion.

Long since had William dissociated himself in feeling from the passionate romance of eight years earlier, and the new attachment being so unlike the old, he slid into a relationship with Mary at once pacifying and encouraging.   Despite Dorothy's absorption in her brother and her fiery tense capacity for divining the very heart of a situation, no jealousies clouded the intercourse of the Sockburn Eden.   It seemed to satisfy Dorothy that as she loved Mary herself William should love her too, what was it but the inevitable outcome of their communal existence?   Never did it enter Dorothy's head to fall in love with either of Mary's brothers, nor does it seem to have occurred to the brothers to pay much attention to their sister's eccentric friend.   Deep seclusion has sometimes proved the nursery of deep passion and the seclusion of the peninsula would today be considered by psychologists almost unnatural and provocative of feelings as volcanic as those developed on Haworth Moor. In the case of Wordsworth this result did not come about, but with Coleridge it was quite otherwise. He had in Germany learnt that life was love and he arrived for his flying visit to Sockburn in an emotionally sensitized condition.

*   *   *   *   *

Wordsworth's friend Joseph Cottle wrote in September from Bristol to announce his intention of exploring the north of England. This delighted the farmhouse party, who welcomed the idea of seeing him again. "If you come down," wrote William, "I will accompany you on your tour. Write to me beforehand. You will come by Greta Bridge, which is about twenty miles from this place. Thither Dorothy and I will go to meet you." Cottle's proposal fitted in well with the Wordsworths' plans, for they had to find another lodging before spring and were considering moving into Cumberland to some place of their own adjacent to a good library.

The scheme as outlined by William did not come off, for Cottle presented himself unannounced at Sockburn one October day with Coleridge at his side. The Wordsworths had last seen their friend at Göttingen, when he was too absorbed in German studies to speak to them; he was now less preoccupied and almost at once began to discuss the fate of their joint venture,

Lyrical Ballads, which had been published and reviewed while both authors had been in Germany. The press had certainly been merciless and critics had jabbed cruelly at the poems. Coleridge had been told by his wife that the *Ballads* were "laughed at and disliked by all with very few excepted," and Wordsworth hazarded the opinion that "the strangeness of *The Ancient Mariner* might have been a handicap to the success of the volume." Nevertheless, it was difficult to account for the malignancy displayed by reviewers, but what was there to be hoped for from strangers when their dear friend Robert Southey had shown neither understanding nor pity and in his density had pronounced *Lyrical Ballads* to be "destitute of merit!" Surely, as Wordsworth said, if he had found himself conscientiously unable to speak well of the book he should have declined the task of reviewing it, for no one knew better than Bob Southey that the poems had been published for bread and bread alone. A few condescending words vaguely praising "talent" would not keep any wolf from any door. "I care little," he added, "for the praise of any professional critic, but as it may help me to bread and butter," and went on petulantly to assert that no motive whatever but pecuniary necessity would ever prevail to commit himself to the press again. All the reviewers were blind to the merits of *The Ancient Mariner*, though a few praised *The Thorn* and *The Idiot Boy*. Dr. Burney, who was fond of comparing poems with old masters, said he could no more regard Wordsworth's rustic verse as poetry than he could look on Turner's compositions as pictures. He praised *Th*

Mad Mother, however, as "an admirable painting in
Michael Angelo's style," and *The Thorn* as being "dark
like a picture by Rembrandt or Spanioletto." Other
critics were kind enough to admire *Tintern Abbey*, but
what Coleridge liked to call the "Conversation Poems"
appealed to on one, and the lyrical quality revealed in
It was the first mild day of March and *I heard a thousand
blended notes* was ignored. Convinced as Dorothy was
of her brother's stature as a poet, she found it hard to
bear up against so dismal a lack of appreciation and
would moan that William's verse would fetch no money
till he had been twenty years in his grave. But for many
a long day she had to submit, as De Quincey records,
to the names of her poets being "trampled underfoot."
Can we wonder that Wordsworth's "aversion from
writing" increased every day?

* * * * *

In the first excitement of re-union the poets were
absorbed in discussion and talked from morn till eve.
As this genial intercourse slackened Coleridge became
aware of Sara Hutchinson's extraordinary power of
attraction. Sara, who was thus suddenly to find herself
beloved by a poet, was a plump little person with fair
skin and fine light brown hair. She was lively, sens-
ible, and plain. Coleridge in his code diary tells how it
befell that one evening while stories were being told
in the flickering firelight he stood in the farm parlour
"holding her hand for a long time, behind her back."
It was then that "love wounded him with a light arrow

99

point poisoned alas and incurable." The rather
commonplace Sara was in a flash transformed into the
ideal "Asra," a being who from henceforth was to be
identified with "all his vanity and all his virtue." In
an instant the tepid jog-trot love of William for Mary
was outshone and two persons who could never hope to
marry became

> Two wedded hearts, if ere were such
> Imprison'd in adjoining cells.

To find that Coleridge had unmistakably enshrined
Sockburn in verse was a delightful discovery to me.
"The statue of the arméd knight," the grey stone in the
cornfield, were safe from earthly corrosion while his
devotion to Asra was immortalized in at least a dozen
poems. To Asra I found *Phantasy* might be referred.

> All look and likeness caught of earth,
> All accident of kin and birth,
> Had passed away. There was no trace
> Of aught on that illumined face,
> Uprais'd beneath the rifted stone,
> But of one spirit all her own;—
> She, she herself, and only she
> Shone through her body visibly.

From Sara he derived "that sort of stirring warmth
about the Heart which is with me the robe of incar-
nation of my genius, such as it is." The romance was
temporarily checked by Wordsworth's insistence that
Coleridge should go with him to Cumberland. Cottle
went too, but left the party at the first stage, Greta
Bridge, and the others tramped on across the Pennines

with John Wordsworth, who had met them at the Bridge Inn.   At Grasmere, Coleridge assisted Wordsworth to make choice of a new home, but as soon as this was settled he went off to do business in Keswick and then hurried back to Sockburn, his heart singing a cheerful lilt:

> When you lov'd me and I loved you,
> Then both of us were born anew.

He may have spent ten or even fourteen days with Asra at the farm, it was long enough to make them associate souls for years to come.   *Love* was composed at this time, a poem Sara was, four weeks later, to see printed in *The Morning Post*.

> All thoughts, all passions, all delights,
> Whatever stirs this mortal frame,
> All are but ministers of love,
>   And feed his sacred flame.

> Oft in my waking dreams do I
> Live o'er again that happy hour,
> When midway on the mount I lay
>   Beside the ruined tower.

> She leant against the arméd man,
> The statue of the armed knight;
> She stood and listened to my lay
>   Amid the lingering light.

> .   .   .   .   .

> I played a soft and doleful air,
> I sang an old and moving story—

An old rude song, that suited well
  That ruin wild and hoary.

   .   .   .   .   .

She listened with a fitting blush,
With downcast eyes and modest grace;
For well she knew, I could not choose
  But gaze upon her face.

Coleridge goes on to tell of his companion's tears of pity and delight.

Her bosom heaved—she stepped aside,
As conscious of my look she stepped—
Then suddenly with timorous eye
  She fled to me and wept.

She half enclosed me with her arms,
She pressed me with a meek embrace;
And bending back her head looked up,
  And gazed upon my face.

'Twas partly love and partly fear,
And partly 'twas a bashful art
That I might rather feel, than see
  The swelling of her heart.

*   *   *   *   *

Under the stimulus of love Coleridge became infused with exquisite sensibility, as his descriptions of simple sights, such as a group of trees or a crowd of flowers by the marge of a river, testify. In setting side by side lines by Coleridge and Wordsworth one gets to recognize the idiosyncrasy of each. Even when they are dealing with the same subjects, for example a circle of hollies forming a bower or retreat, there is no mistaking the authorship.

> I sat within an undergrove
> Of tallest hollies, tall and green
> A fairer bower was never seen.
> From year to year the spacious floor
> With withered leaves is covered o'er,
> And all the year the bower is green,

wrote one poet, while the other mused:

> Within these circling hollies, woodbine clad—
> Beneath this small blue roof of vernal sky—
> How warm, how still!   Tho' tears should dim mine eye
> Yet will my heart for days continue glad,
> For here, my love, thou art, and here am I!

Wordsworth's brisk, bleak narrative manner wakes no echo of music in the mind, but Coleridge leaves us with a glowing melody.

*   *   *   *   *

Before William got back to Sockburn, Coleridge had vanished, as he had work to do for *The Morning Post* in London.   Dorothy and Sara had seen him on his road, as was their way with departing guests, and William, writing in that odd dry way of his, said:

> I scarcely knew whether to be sorry or not that you were no longer here, it would have been a great pain for me to have parted with you. . . .   I was sadly disappointed in not finding Dorothy.   Mary was a solitary housekeeper and overjoyed to see me.

He had much to tell Dorothy, for he had found just the right house for a home. It was an old panelled cottage on the edge of Grasmere known as Town-end. It had been an inn, "The Dove and Olive Bough," but from henceforth its wainscoted walls were to be the setting for a poet's life, the scene of tireless industry. Wordsworth was to describe it later on in *The Waggoner*:

> There where the Dove and Olive Bough
> Once hung, a Poet harbours now
> A simple water-drinking Bard.

Mary Hutchinson had also a tale to tell, for she was worried over Coleridge's obviously deep feeling for Sara and could not anticipate that with almost unnatural discretion he had decided to make no trouble for them by confiding his passion to notebooks and cypher alone. It is only through the transcription of these data that we know how overwhelming was the emotional effect of the Sockburn visit.

* * * * *

When autumn came with short days, absence of flowers, foliage and birds, William began taking an interest in sport by watching, since there was nothing else to watch, the Hutchinson brothers coursing hares. The dogs that had barked at his coming were now old friends, and he was so moved by the drowning of one of the greyhounds, Dart, and by the consequent behaviour of his favourite beagle Music, that he wrote verses on the morning's sport.

WORDSWORTH AT SOCKBURN

On his morning round the Master
Goes to learn how all things fare;
Searches pasture after pasture,
Sheep and cattle eyes with care;
And, for silence or for talk,
He hath comrades in his walk;
Four dogs, each pair of different breed,
Distinguished, two for scent and two for speed.

See a hare before him started!
—Off they fly in earnest chase;
Every dog is eager-hearted,
All the four are in the race;
And the hare whom they pursue
Knows from instinct what to do;
Her hope is near: no turn she makes;
But like an arrow to the river takes.

Deep the river was, and crusted
Thinly by a one night's frost;
But the nimble hare hath trusted
To the ice and safely crost;
All are following at full speed,
When lo! the ice so thinly spread,
Breaks—and the greyhound, Dart, is overhead!

Better fate have Prince and Swallow,
See them cleaving to the sport!
Music has no heart to follow,
Little Music she stops short.
She hath neither wish nor heart,
Hers is now another part:
A loving creature she and brave!
And fondly strives her friend to save.

From the brink her paws she stretches
Very hands as you would say!
And afflicting moans she fetches,
As he breaks the ice away.
For herself she hath no fears—
Him alone she sees and hears,—
Makes efforts with complainings; nor gives o'er
Until her fellow sinks to reappear no more.

"Little Music" was never forgotten, and when she died six years later, Wordsworth wrote a tribute to her memory.

*   *   *   *   *

The Wordsworths having made up their minds to leave Sockburn for a house of their own were not altogether reluctant to rise from their beds one December morning, mount the horses that George Hutchinson had brought to the door, and ride down to the ford. Dorothy was enchanted with the way the Tees glittered in the frosty moonlight. Ten miles of hacking through Yorkshire brought them to the Swale spoken of by Dorothy as "a beautiful river with its green bank and flat holms scattered over with trees." By Richmond and its "ivied castle," the tower of which looked to them like "a huge steeple," they journeyed on to Wensleydale. Here George Hutchinson abandoned them and returned to Sockburn with the horses, while Dorothy and William braced themselves to trudge on another ten miles to Askrigg, where they intended to rest for the night. Much of the walk was accomplished in snow and careful descriptions were registered by Dorothy of waterfalls, "congealed froth," "incumbent rocks," "reflected lights on streams and clouds," all of which were meant to be of use to William. On the 18th of December they slept at Sedbergh, on the 19th at Kendal, and next day on reaching Grasmere they took possession of a partly furnished and unaired house, the chimneys of which smoked badly. It was a cheerless Christmas even for people to whom as a festival it meant nothing at all. Both Wordsworths caught bad colds and Dorothy was racked by toothache. William alluded to this pain as "a grievous misfortune,"since it held up needlework on bed-curtains and other protective comforts. Ready as always to put a good face on a bad job, and the cottage in the beginning was certainly a bad job, Dorothy fell to praising the orchard and wrestling with the kitchen fire. From this time on, the ex-inn on the outskirts of Grasmere became the Wordsworths' home. After they had ceased to live in it, it was renamed Dove Cottage, and under that title is known to countless sightseers.

When the move had sunk below the level of consciousness it rose again as a poeticized memory to be described in *The Recluse.*

> Bleak season was it, turbulent and bleak
> When hitherward we journeyed side by side
> Through bursts of sunshine and through flying showers;
> Paced the long vales—how long they were—and yet
> How fast that length of way was left behind,
> Wensley's rich Vale, and Sedbergh's naked heights.
> The frosty wind, as if to make amends

For its keen breath, was aiding to our steps,
And drove us onward like two ships at sea,
Or like two birds, companions in mid-air
Parted and reunited by the blast.
Stern was the face of nature; we rejoiced
In that stern countenance, for our souls thence drew
A feeling of their strength.   The naked trees,
The icy brooks, as on we passed, appeared
To question us.   "Whence come ye, to what end?"
They seemed to say.   "What would ye," said the shower,
"Wild wanderers, whither through my dark domain?"
The sunbeam said, "Be happy."   When this vale
We entered, bright and solemn was the sky
That faced us with a passionate welcoming,
And led us to our threshold.   Daylight failed
Insensibly, and round us gently fell
Composing darkness, with a quiet load
Of full contentment, in a little shed
Disturbed, uneasy in itself as seemed,
And wondering at its new inhabitants.
It loves us now, this Vale so beautiful
Begins to love us!

In my many walks to Sockburn I sometimes, like the Wordsworths, approached it from the Yorkshire bank, crossing the Tees by a wire bridge.   In this way one got the same impression of the farm as they did on the day of their arrival.   A road from Neasham, made I suppose when Sockburn Hall was built, is now the usual approach to the peninsula, and it amuses me to think how indignant William Wordsworth would have been that his paradise should be profaned by wheeled traffic, and how he would have resented the big stone mansion in Abbotsford Gothic to which the road leads!

SOCKBURN CHURCH, *circa* 1807

To him it would have appeared as a monstrous inter-
ference with the amenities of paradise, but in his day
the Hall had not been thought of nor in 1799 had
the idea of bridging the Tees been projected. These
changes were set afoot in 1833, and it is evident that it
was the intention of the rich man, who built the house,
to supersede the ford that led to Entercommon by
constructing on the same spot a bridge for vehicles.
For some reason the structure was never completed; its
ends are in the void and suspended between them is a
light wire footbridge. The builder of the Hall had the
temerity to remove from the chapel to the house "the
statue of the arméd knight," and he also reduced the
church to the diminished ruin it is today. In order
to protect his personal privacy from the observation
of a few worshippers, he of his bounty provided
another building, far less commodious, for their de-
votions. It was situated a mile down-stream on a
cliff on the far side of the river, and farmers on the
peninsula had to make use of a ferry-boat to attend
the services.

Another family now owns Sockburn Hall and has
very properly restored the knight to his chapel. The
Hall in its solidity blocks out a reach of the river and
claims the peninsula as a setting for itself. But no
nineteenth-century mansion, however imposing, can
cause one to forget that Sockburn stands for more than
the expression of material prosperity: it stands for England itself and that older, deeper-rooted life that I
should like to be instrumental in preserving. Sockburn is a blesséd place in which a poet was inspired to

write lines that have passed into the language of our race.

> The outward things of sky and earth
> Of hill and valley he has viewed
> And impulses of deeper birth
> Have come to him in solitude.

> In common things that round us lie
> Some random truths he can impart
> The harvest of the quiet eye
> That broods and sleeps on its own heart.

At Sockburn Wordsworth found the key to plenitude and peace, and Coleridge a love that was to form the undersong of his life.

SEQUEL TO SOCKBURN

SEQUEL TO SOCKBURN

FOR over two years William and Dorothy lived contentedly in their Town-end cottage which became for them "the loved abode." Front garden, orchard, Indian shed, shrubs, Dorothy's stone-flagged bedroom and William's warm study all were indued by their owners with ideal qualities. At first roses and honeysuckles had not grown quickly enough to satisfy Dorothy so she had trained "scarlet beans upon Threads" to clothe the cottage walls to the eaves. Sharing to the full the taste of the age for creepers, moss-grown stones and dripping grottos, she felt, as did so many of her contemporaries, that the closer one could muffle one's house and one's policies with verdure, the cosier and serener life became. Scott in his bee-hive cottage at Lasswade had also enjoyed training jasmine, honeysuckle, and roses over the porch and up the walls and lesser folk all over the country followed suit. This to me quite horrid form of rusticity was the aftermath of Rousseau's back to nature teaching and a concession to the sentimentality of an age that derived a kind of regeneration from natural contacts. It is not so easy to enter into the mind of the time, partly because the poets apprehended Nature in such differing ways. Coleridge felt her as a force coursing through his veins, a power enhancing his vitality. Wordsworth regarded Nature as a refuge from the troubles of the time, as a pacifying and reassuring influence. God was in Nature, and from Nature "moments of imaginative energy" could with patience be wooed. Since the visible universe provided to William the clearest evidence of God there was a moral value in communion with mountains, lakes, clouds, for man's ennoblement could only be achieved by mergence with the inanimate. Wordsworth spoke of "grand and permanent forms" in which the wisdom and spirit of the universe seemed most unmistakably manifest. With Nature he felt his better self to be uppermost. In her company

> The master current of his brain
> Ran permanent and free.

In her presence he was consumed by no morbid passion, no disquietude. On the contrary he derived a sense of holy peace from his retirement and felt the bond between the soul of Nature and the soul of man to be the greatest reality of all.

If a poet may be defined, as Wordsworth lays down, as "a man pleased with his own passions and volitions and who rejoices more than other men in the spirit of life that is in him," it may be added that when the flame of his spirit fades he may have to depend on someone else to coax it back into incandescence. This waiting on the wind of the spirit obliged the Wordsworths to keep unpractical, capricious hours, for sometimes there was the will but not the mood to write. In complete surrender of self Dorothy would sit up with her brother till four in the morning or walk to and fro with him in the cold moonlight "to help him," as she would say, simply "to warm up to his work."

Under the encouragement of the woman whose voice "reminded him of a hidden bird," the starkly veridical personality that was William Wordsworth would kindle into a state of imaginative perception which might flare into creation or might merely flicker into composition. The making of poetry was admittedly a great nervous strain and the act of writing exhausted the poet so much physically that afterwards he had to be cosseted like a sick man. He was enormously dependant on his womenfolk, those women who wrote of him to each other as "our own dear love." Though the fitful presence of Coleridge was highly stimulating to William, always in the background of his mind there was Dorothy, who, Coleridge or no Coleridge, never failed her brother. Instinctively she knew when he was so far launched upon his work as no longer to need her at his side. She then would be free for household ploys and pleasures such as reading *Henry V* aloud to herself in the orchard, writing to her dear friend Jane Clarkson, or even to William's old love Annette Vallon.

The poems assigned to the first two years' occupation of Town-end are numerous. Those composed in "the orchard" seem less good than others labelled "Town-end." Faithful to the belief that poetic diction should be taken from common speech, that is to say, language as really used by men, and that poetry should reflect nature, William listened to the slow talk of the countryside and laboured to reproduce its simplicity. He would go so far as deliberately to sacrifice the precise word to the plainer word. From Dorothy's notes we see that work was in progress on *The Pedlar*, *The Singing Bird*, *Alice Fell*, *The Beggar Boy*, *To a Butterfly*, *To a small Celandine*, and *The Leech-gatherer*, a rather unimaginative commonplace bunch of poems. Had William perhaps carried the cult of plainness too far? Was it not time to break through the entangling net of wild flowers, birds and butterflies, the recording of nature and recapture that deeper sensibility and emotion divorced from which his poetry, despite the high import he attributed to everything he wrote, became without significance.

Even the family circle rebelled against some of his duller verses. Sara Hutchinson ventured to object to *The Leech-gatherer*. She had found it tedious and William wrote to her explaining that everything is tedious when one does not read it with the feelings of the author. "Why, *The Thorn* is tedious to hundreds, and so is *The Idiot Boy*!" To these words Dorothy appends a postscript telling Sara, "when you feel any poem of his to be tedious, ask yourself in what spirit it was written—whether merely to tell the tale and be through with it or to illustrate a particular character or truth." Of *The Idiot Boy* he used to say, "I never wrote anything with so much glee." To me the owl verses are the only tolerable ones in the whole poem.

> The owlets through the long blue night,
> Are shouting to each other still:
> Fond lovers! yet not quite hob-nob,
> They lengthen out the tremulous sob,
> That echoes far from hill to hill.

* * * * * *

The owls have hooted all night long,
And with the owls began my song,
And with the owls must end.

The Thorn has a quality of extreme complacency and banality and the story of the woman in the scarlet cloak and the infant's grave seems to me a trumped-up effort at pathos that is almost nauseating. Sometimes these simpler anecdotic poems were tried out on country folk. "We have our hair-cutter below stairs, William is reading *The Leech-gatherer* to him," writes Dorothy. I do not find dissatisfaction expressed either by Wordsworth or his sister at anything written at this time, though Dorothy certainly thought more highly of some poems than of others.

* * * * *

During the first three months the Wordsworths were at Town-end, Coleridge was pinned down in London working for *The Morning Post* and completing a contract for Longman. Charles Lamb, with whom he stayed in Pentonville for three weeks in March, wrote describing his guest as wrapped in dressing-gown and looking like a conjuror as he fagged away at the, to him, disgusting task of translating two of Schiller's plays, *The Piccolomini* and *The Death of Wallenstein*. Longman paid him £50 and was to lose money on the book, the pages of which were said to have become "winding-sheets for pilchards." As soon as he had finished his task and thrown up his work for *The Morn-*

ing Post, Coleridge, according to Charles Lamb, bolted off "on a visit to his god Wordsworth." At Grasmere he was an exceedingly welcome guest, though harassed beyond measure as to how to plan his life. Should he live in Ottery to please Poole? or in Bristol to please his wife and Cottle? There were insurmountable objections to both courses because he must be near Wordsworth, and Wordsworth would not budge from Town-end. The merits of Keswick were considered. It was neither too near nor too far from Grasmere and the matter was clenched when Dorothy undertook to arrange for the Coleridge family a part tenancy of Greta Hall, a new house with a fine view belonging to their friend Mr. Jackson, the Waggoner. Coleridge, pacified in mind, went to Bristol (May 4) with the intention of transporting his household to Keswick during the summer. When he was gone, William and John Wordsworth set off for Gallow Hill, to visit the farm in which Thomas Hutchinson had settled himself with Mary. The Hutchinson family had now broken up and George was living with Sara in a farm at Bishop's Middleham. Thomas's farm was near Brompton in the North Riding of Yorkshire, and William on his return must have contrasted it unfavourably with Sockburn, for we catch Dorothy registering a vow that she "would never go to Gallow Hill," a vow she was later on forced to break.

In the closing days of June, long after Dorothy expected them, the Coleridges and their little son Hartley arrived at Town-end. To his host Coleridge seemed ominously ill. The migrants stayed for nearly a month and then moved in to Greta Hall, the exterior of which promised a degree of comfort which the interior denied. Even the view from the windows did not prevent Coleridge from realizing how badly built, damp, and draughty the house was. Thirteen miles from Town-end and Coleridge frequently was able, in spite of constant indisposition, to walk over Dunmail Raise to see his friends. At Christmas-time he was taken ill at Grasmere with a bout of rheumatic fever. Sara Hutchinson happened to be at Town-end too, and as they could not help enjoying each other's company, the aches and pains were easy to bear. Not so easy was it for Coleridge to return to his wife, but *à contre cœur* he did so only to be bedridden once more under less favourable conditions at Greta. It was during this illness that he began to take the "Kendal black drop," that acted on him like a charm.

In July he went to Durham professedly to read Duns Scotus in the Cathedral library. Here he was within easy reach of George Hutchinson's farm, where Sara was to be visited, and it seems that he spent turn and turn about a night or two at Durham and a night or two at the farm. He was suffering a good deal from a swollen knee and when the doctor recommended sea-water treatment he seized on the chance offered him by Sara of riding with her to Gallow Hill, which was seven miles short of Scarborough. At Scarborough he bathed in the open sea and enjoyed an extreme richness of sensation, the emotional well-being that one learns to associate with the companionship of Asra. In the Schiller manner he enters into the joy of the universe and in beatific mood feels that what no one shares with him is scarce his own. A pæan composed on the beach at Scarborough brings to mind the chorus in the Ninth Symphony:

> God be with thee, gladsome Ocean!
> How gladly greet I thee once more!
> Ships and waves, and ceaseless motion,
> And men rejoicing on thy shore.
>
> Me a thousand hopes and pleasures,
> A thousand recollections bland,
> Thoughts sublime and stately measures,
> Revisit on thy echoing strand.
>
> Dreams (the Soul herself forsaking),
> Tearful raptures, boyish mirth;
> Silent adorations making
> A blessed shadow of this earth!
>
> Oh ye hopes that stir within me,
> Health comes with you from above,
> God is with me, God is in me!
> I cannot die, if Life be Love.

At Göttingen he had learnt to understand and love the *Ausgelassenheit* of Schiller's verse, which was intensely congenial to him in a way that the plays were not, and one hears the sympathetic echo frequently of lines like this:

> Freude heisst die starke Feder
> In der ewigen Natur.
> Freude, Freude, treibt die Räder
> In der grossen Weltenuhr.

Blumen lockt sie aus dem Keimen,
Sonnen aus dem Firmament,
Sphären rollt sie in dem Räumen,
Die des Sehers Rohr nicht kennt.

Sometimes in floriferous enjoyment he would sing;

Flowers are lovely; Love is flowerlike,
Friendship is a sheltering tree.
Oh! the joys that come down showerlike
Of Friendship, Love and Liberty.

As he often said, it is not time itself that counts for anything, what matters is what transpires in the flying hours.   Coleridge was deeply aware that his whole life had been altered by that short, fatal visit to Sockburn: an equally short stay at Gallow Hill enabled him to enjoy an æon of delight.

It was with resentment in his heart that he returned to his family at Keswick.   Home life was less and less tolerable, indeed he was so unhappy that he found it impossible to work at Greta Hall.   And yet if his family were to live he must work and work hard.   If only he could lodge apart from them!   To mitigate his spiritual isolation he tried to persuade Southey (who paid him a visit at Greta in August) to come and winter with him at Keswick, but Southey flitted off to a secretarial post in Dublin.   After an autumn spent in oscillation between Greta Hall and Town-end, Coleridge escaped south.   He spent Christmas at Stowey and January and February in London.   On one of the first days of March 1802 he again visited Gallow Hill and by the 19th was at Grasmere primed once more to write

in the lush Schiller spirit. His opulence of emotion
vented itself in outpourings like *A Daydream*,

> O ever—ever be thou blest!
> For dearly Asra! I love thee!
> This brooding warmth across my breast
> This depth of tranquil bliss—ah me!

and *The Picture* with its exquisite lines about the love-
distempered youth,

> Who ne'er henceforth may see an aspen-grove
> Shiver in sunshine, but his feeble heart
> Shall flow away like a dissolving thing.

All the happiness drawn from Gallow Hill is in these
poems; he has somehow bottled the sunshine and the
magic still glows. Always, until the breach eight years
later, Sara had the power of suffusing him with the
glowing emotion that forced itself to expression in
verse.

*   *   *   *   *

Since the walks at Alfoxden in 1797 there had been
no common effusion of creative energy, consequent on
the poets being together, but in March 1802 a similar
phenomenon recurred. During the last days of the
month Coleridge and Wordsworth were together under
one roof. Coleridge, full of radiance and plenitude,
talked the waking hours away and miracle of miracles
Wordsworth was delivered from the snares of nature
observation into a wider æther. The first four stanzas
of what some have called the greatest poem in our
language were written, *Ode on Intimations of Immortality.*

We can but connect the revivification of Wordsworth's diviner faculties with the companionship of Coleridge. The poets acted upon each other as tinder and flint and within the week two deathless Odes had been given form, the *Ode on Immortality* and the *Ode on Dejection*.

In the *Intimations* Wordsworth laments that he is no longer able to experience the ineffable, and this personal discovery is transmuted into the universal experience, the journey of man away from the East. The verses were written at Town-end on the 27th of March 1802 and the following day William, Dorothy and Coleridge tramped off to Greta Hall, where on the 4th of April the *Ode to Dejection* was composed. The Schillerian note is still dominant and in the manuscript preserved at Grasmere the word "Lady" had not yet been substituted for "Sara."

> O Sara! we receive but what we give
> And in our life alone does Nature live;
> Ours is her wedding garment, ours her shroud.

From Keswick William walked on to Bishop's Middleham to make arrangements for his marriage with Mary Hutchinson, while Dorothy and Coleridge wandered back to Town-end, where Coleridge read his *Ode* aloud to Dorothy. She alludes to it as "the verses he wrote to Sara" and was so affected by them as to fall into "miserable spirits." Both William and Dorothy were still deeply apprehensive about their friend's attachment to Sara and what might be the eventual outcome of their love. In his new poem Coleridge laments being robbed of mirth and of his birthright—

"the shaping spirit of Imagination," the spirit that caused Edgar Allen Poe to tremble in reading Coleridge's poetry.

*   *   *   *   *

It was three years since William and Mary had agreed to marry each other. They had been lean years and perhaps it was the promise of Lord Lonsdale's heir to repay a loan of some £8,500 owing to the Wordsworth family that now made the future safe for matrimony. It would seem that Dorothy was by far more interested in her brother's old love Annette than William himself. For nine years she had maintained with this unknown Frenchwoman a desultory correspondence. Now that preparations for a wedding were on foot something she was sure ought to be done about William's child. She must see how things turned out, but would enter in her diary the resolve "to see Annette." The more she thought things over, the less could she relinquish her desire to clear up the French entanglement: the road to France was open for the first time for ten years, the recently signed peace of Amiens made it possible for English people once more to visit the Continent. In discussing the project with William, Dorothy was probably actuated by a sense of duty and it is just possible that Annette was in need of the financial help which for the first time William could afford to offer. William proving amenable to her suggestion, Dorothy laid plans for meeting Annette at Calais as soon as convenient.

By July the Wordsworths were ready to set out on their journey with the double objective, that of breaking with the old love and marrying the new. To quit Grasmere at all proved for William a great uprooting. He felt constrained to write an apology to his garden for leaving "the loveliest spot that man has ever found" and "the blesséd life" which it distressed him to interrupt even for two months.

> We go for One to whom ye will be dear;
> And she will prize this Bower, this Indian shed,
> Our own contrivance, Building without peer!
> —A gentle Maid, whose heart is lowly bred,
> Whose pleasures are in wild fields gathered,
> With joyousness and with a thoughtful cheer,
> Will come to you; to you herself will wed;
> And love the blesséd life that we lead here.
>
> . . . .
>
> Help us to tell Her tales of years gone by,
> And this sweet spring, the best beloved and best;
> Joy will be flown in its mortality;
> Something must stay to tell us of the rest.
> Here thronged with primroses, the steep rock's breast
> Glittered at evening like a starry sky;
> And in this bush our sparrow built her nest,
> Of which I sang one song that will not die.
> O happy Garden! whose seclusion deep
> Hath been so friendly to industrious hours;
> And to soft slumbers, that did gently steep
> Our spirits, carrying them dreams of flowers,
> And wild notes warbled among leafy bowers;
> Two burning months let summer overleap,
> And coming back with Her who will be ours
> Into thy bosom we again shall creep.

From Grasmere they went to Greta Hall for the week-end. Mrs. Coleridge, who hated living in the north, complained as usual of having no friends there and of the climate and the badly built house. Dorothy, a little out of patience, alluded to her as "a sad fiddle-faddler" and "the lightest, weakest, silliest woman and moreover so insensitive and irritable that she could not come to any good."

Coleridge, loth to part with his quests, walked on with them to Eusemire, the new-built house of Thomas and Jane Clarkson. After two nights at Eusemire the travellers took the coach at Emont Bridge and drove in it by Stainmoor over "Gaterley Moor," a "glorious ride, every building was bathed in golden light . . ." "The trees were more bright than earthly trees and we saw," wrote Dorothy of her stereoscopic vision, "round us for miles upon miles." At Leeming Lane they spent a night, then hiring a post-chaise hurried on in dawn-light to breakfast at Thirsk. To savour the summer day to the full they consigned their luggage to a carrier and went on foot the rest of the way.

Dorothy headed eagerly for Rievaulx, she generally forged ahead with William in her wake, and having rambled about the Abbey ruins insisted that her brother before going to Helmsley should climb up to "Mr. Duncombe's terrace" for the view. At Helmsley they put up at the Black Swan with its yellow walls and its casements wreathed with jasmine. The jasmine has been cut away, but the afternoon sun still irradiates the walls and the windows on the market-place. The

kitchen hearth, by which the travellers sat that evening and again some weeks later on the afternoon of
William's wedding day, may be seen by any curious
visitor, but of the floors "smooth as ice" alluded to by
Dorothy I saw no trace.

From Helmsley the Wordsworths walked on to
Kirkby Moorside, talking by the way of the gay Duke of
Buckingham and the miserable end that overtook him
there.   From Kirkby the ground drops seaward to the
south, and as they emerged from the folds of the hills at
Pickering they looked over the fertile flats leading to
Brompton, their destination.   Seven miles short of
Gallow Hill they were greeted by Mary and Sara
Hutchinson.

Dorothy's curiosity about Gallow Hill had been
stimulated by Coleridge's accounts of his radiant visits
there.   As the party neared their destination and
walked up the avenue of trees leading from Brompton
church to the farm, she could see peeping up at the back
the hill from which it derived its grisly title.   It was
just a grass hill dominating the turnpike and had been
one of the execution centres of 1568, a place where
Catholics after the Rising of the Northern Earls had
been strung up as a lesson to passers-by.   They talked a
little of old times as happy people will and someone said
that in Percy's *Reliques* there was a ballad about the
Rising and the part played in it by old Norton and his
eight sons.   It may be that from these careless words
was sown the seed in Wordsworth's mind of a poem
that was to germinate later as *The White Doe*.   When I
first saw the grassy contours of the hill they were

rippling with daffodils. The hill had as new a face as the farm which had been rebuilt after a fire in which outhouses alone had survived destruction.

As I stood on the summit looking towards the village church I saw that such significance as had attached to it had vanished with the diversion of the high road. Even the avenue of trees that once shaded the path from farm to church had suffered loss: a few survivors stood in fields, the rest had gone. Every sentimental association has been ironed out; it is just possible that in Wordsworth's day memories of old and passionate partisanship lingered about the place.

I do not know when Wordsworth first read in Percy's *Reliques* "The Rising of the North," but having experienced how strangely ideas jump together in one's subconsciousness, even though separated by time and place, it may be that the story of Gallow Hill, linked up as it was by the Hutchinsons with the whole story of the Rising, may have lain incubating in William's mind until called to life by a visit to Bolton Priory five years later, the visit that caused him to begin work on *The White Doe*. We know that he regarded the story of Norton and his eight sons, killed in the Rising, as "of epic quality," and was furious when the industriously antiquarian Scott told him that he could furnish proof that Norton had really escaped abroad. Refusing to pay heed to this offer, he said tradition was good enough for him, and produced a poem containing jingling rhymes that challenged comparison with Scott's own narratives in verse. *The White Doe* is said to have been completed under the lee of a haystack at Stockton-on-

Tees. Persuaded by Coleridge's assurance that the poem would be ill-received, Wordsworth put the verses away in a cupboard where they lay for eight years.

*　　*　　*　　*　　*

Ten days were spent at this time by the Wordsworths at Gallow Hill. Both families were in agreement that no wedding should take place until William had had the opportunity of interviewing his former mistress, and of at least offering to adopt or partially support his own daughter.

On a morning of soft summer rain William and Dorothy left Gallow Hill in a post-chaise. Mary, as was her way, drove off with them, but dismounted short of Beverley. By way of Hull and Lincoln the travellers reached London and at Charing Cross climbed on to the Dover coach. "It was a beautiful morning," noted Dorothy as they crossed the Thames. "The city, St. Paul's with the river and a multitude of little boats made a most beautiful sight." Brother and sister were quivering with emotion and excitement and capable of almost any imaginative flight. What we apprehend of William's method of work, and what we know of the genesis of certain sets of verse, goes to show that Dorothy was usually the quickest to perceive beauty, that she would communicate her vision to her brother in whose mind it lay till fecundated by his imagination. By the date of their return her observations on leaving London had been transmuted into

Ships, towers, domes, theatres and temples lie
Open unto the fields, and to the sky,
All bright and glistening in the smokeless air.

At Calais Annette Vallon and her girl, Caroline,
awaited them with we know not what feelings of curiosity and sentiment.   Of the meeting itself we have no
record, but it was followed by four weeks of companionship and William, as we see clearly in the sonnets
that date from this moment, was once more experiencing
genuine, spontaneous feeling.   The sight of his own
child, unresponsive though she seemed, caught at his
heart,

Dear Child! dear Girl! that walkest with me here,
If thou appear untouched by solemn thought,
Thy nature is not therefore less divine.

The sonnet in which these lines occur and eight other
sonnets were the fruits of the visit to France.   At last,
as Dorothy rejoiced to see, he had broken loose from the
rustic obsessions of Grasmere and he had regained the
mind's initiative, imagination.   Was it possible that
marriage would do less for his creative faculty than
Annette had done and could still do?   This to her was
the great question.

*   *   *   *   *

To understand the anomalous though somehow
gratifying situation in which William and Dorothy had
now placed themselves we must go back ten years
and look at Wordsworth in January 1791 when he left

Cambridge. He was without plans for the future though his uncle had offered to give him "a title for Holy Orders." Because of his inner conviction that "to vegetate in a paltry curacy" would be insupportable, he temporized over the proposal, saying he would accept the offer when it proved most convenient. All professions to his mind were "attended with great inconveniences," but that of the priesthood with the most. Had he only known it, Southey and Coleridge, later to become his friends, were in the same predicament. From Cambridge he went to London, where he picked up some sort of a livelihood. In *The Prelude* he says:

> I ranged at large through London's wide domain
> Month after month. Obscurely did I live
> Not seeking frequent intercourse with men
> By literature, or elegance or rank
> Distinguished.

Everyone in England was talking of the Revolution in France. Wherever men congregated the subject was discussed. Hearing first one opinion and then another, William decided to see how things were for himself, he would cross to France. From Brighton he sailed for Dieppe and four days later was in Paris. The city seemed less upset than he expected, in fact it was quiet and dull. No thrills could he achieve by running round to pick a stone from the Bastille or by visiting the new temple of St. Genevieve, or the Jacobin Club, or by being introduced (by a deputy) to the National Assembly. Could the Revolution already have fizzled out? Was this the new world order?

Uncertain of the trend of affairs, he went on to

Orleans ostensibly to learn good French and there boarded at the same lodging as three cavalry officers. Lonely at first and given to solitary walks, he was discovered by Annette Vallon, a surgeon's daughter, who offered to teach him French. In her company week after week "stole insensibly" over his head "with inconceivable rapidity." Love revealed to him in Annette's company undreamt-of depths of feeling and happiness. As lovers they moved to Blois to be less observed and there William found in Michael de Beaupuy a friend with whom to discuss political theory, "civil government" and the "voluptuous atmosphere of royal courts" where "the man who is of soul the meanest thrives the most." Suddenly he develops into "a patriot," his whole "heart given to the people." With deep emotion he watches "*les enfants de la patrie*" marching to the frontier in defence of Liberty." How can anyone believe that invaders, even if they were to succeed in reaching the gates of Paris, could put the clock back?

> All institutes for ever blotted out
> That legalized exclusion, empty pomp
> Abolished, sensual state and cruel power
> Whether by edict of the one or few;
> And finally as sum and crown of all
> Should see the people having a strong hand
> In framing their own laws; whence better days
> To all mankind.

In this glowing atmosphere the awkward immature student became a man, and began to talk and to write with a hitherto unexperienced facility. His love for

Annette bursts through his verse and in *Vaudracour and Julia* we may see how illumined and tender he of a sudden became.   Like all lovers of those days he read to his mistress the romantic plays of Shakespeare and in them found surprising expression of his feelings. He could endorse the very words of Romeo and Lorenzo: life took on the tempo of a rhapsody.

> Oh, happy time of youthful lovers,
> O balmy time
> In which a love-knot on a lady's brow
> Is fairer than the fairest star in Heaven.

Verses poured themselves out naturally, no invention was exercised for none was needed.   Annette seemed to make all things plain and all things easy.   Wordsworth's mind, steeped in Shakespearean verse, threw off lines like these:

> Arabian fiction never filled the world
> With half the wonders that were wrought for him.
> Earth breathed in one great presence of the spring;
> Life turned the meanest of her implements
> Before his eyes, to price above all gold;
> The house she dwelt in was a sainted shrine;
> Her chamber windows did surpass in glory
> The portals of the dawn; all paradise
> Could by the simple opening of a door
> Let itself in upon him:—pathways, walks,
> Swarmed with enchantment, till his spirit sank,
> Surcharged, within him, overblest to move
> Beneath a sun that wakes a weary world
> To its dull round of ordinary cares;
> A man too happy for mortality.

Never was this effulgent experience to be renewed. Never again was Wordsworth to escape so completely from his own confining and rather difficult character.

*　　*　　*　　*　　*

Love for Annette did not blind William to the political situation in France. The structure of society was changing. The very men he was associated with were

> . . . called upon to exercise their skill
> Not in Utopia, subterranean fields,
> Or some secreted island, Heaven knows where!
> But in the very world, which, which is the world
> Of all of us,—the place where in the end
> We find our happiness or not at all!

Wordsworth faced up to the questions of the hour: Was Kingship to be abolished? Was the Golden Age dawning? Would France, once the Constitution were adopted, renounce for ever the monarchical lust for conquest? Would not a people in arms obedient to officers of its own election be more than a match for the hired legions of any despotic power? These were the conundrums of the hour.

When Wordsworth learnt of Louis XVI's flight to Varennes, of the enforced return, of the sack of the Tuileries, he wondered what men at home were thinking. What would be England's attitude towards the newly proclaimed Republic? Pitt, it seemed, was rigidly neutral and yet the British ambassador had been withdrawn from Paris. What ought an Englishman in

France to do? What must a patriot think? Must he abandon happiness, must he offer to fight?

If Wordsworth had but known it, there were numbers of Englishmen who, though they were neither living in France nor in love with a French girl, welcomed the new dispensation and felt as Wordsworth did that it was the dawn of a new day for humanity. Lord Lansdowne, for example, professed himself a Jacobin: Lord Sempill of the 3rd Guards and Lord Edward Fitzgerald of the 54th Regiment openly subscribed to the Republican cause. England, it was said, was honeycombed with Jacobin clubs.

William and Annette had been constrained by prospective parenthood to return to Orleans in July. Three months before the baby's birth they may be seen indulging their fond sensibility. Annette is making baby-clothes: she hands out the tiny pink bonnet for her William to kiss. Their love is still an idyll. Now comes the surprise. But one short month passes and Annette has been inexplicably abandoned. Many reasons have been put forward to explain William's action; none is convincing. Some have said that he got into political entanglements, others that he went away in order to arrange to be married before the baby's birth. Wordsworth's nephew and first biographer, Christopher Wordsworth, who possibly may have destroyed the evidence that proved it, said that William, while abroad, was intimately connected with the Brissotins. It is believed that he identified himself sufficiently with Republicans to have attended a civic feast

135

held in Orleans in celebration of the fall of the Monarchy. This took place in September 1791, and in October he was in Paris. There he remained for two months, which seems to undercut the notion that he left Annette in order to speed up his marriage. It was in Paris that he heard of the birth of his child, but in spite of his devotion to its mother he did not return to Orleans, nor did he see his daughter at all till she was ten years old.

The baby was christened at the Cathedral church of Sainte Croix shortly before Christmas, receiving the names of Anne Caroline Wordsworth, daughter of William Wordsworth, "Anglois," and Marie Anne Vallon. "Dragged," as he alleges, "by a train of harsh necessity," the young father returned to England. Perhaps he was penniless, perhaps a fit of circumspection dictated that he should secure the consent of his guardians before taking an irrevocable step, perhaps it was mere evasion of responsibility, perhaps his views on marriage changed when he came under Godwin's influence. Whatever the reason that caused him to act as he did, it does not seem to harmonize very well with all the passion experienced so short a while before. Annette's letters go to show that William had promised to come and fetch her when he had got a little money together and had overcome his relations' inevitable disapproval of his conduct abroad. Dorothy, who was of course in all his secrets, was deputed to create a favourable atmosphere for him with his maternal uncle, Canon Cookson, who lived at Windsor. The Canon, unwilling to condone his nephew's behaviour, was also unwilling to admit the culprit to his house. Almost before William could turn round to look for help elsewhere, war was declared between England and France, and plans for returning to France, if any existed, had to be laid aside. The scandal, for such it appeared to Canon Cookson and other members of the family, was now hushed up, and that so efficiently that it is only within the last twenty years that the facts have become generally known. Dorothy, with extraordinary fairmindedness and understanding, began and kept up a correspondence with Annette. Annette in her turn wrote constantly to her lover, but few of these missives reached him, or so it is thought. The French girl praised Dorothy for her unique goodness and expressed the hope that Caroline might resemble her. Caroline is sweet and daily grows more and more like "papa." On no account must "*le plus chéri des hommes*" run the risk of being taken prisoner in France. One day she knows that her lover will come back.

When he was an old man Wordsworth told Carlyle that he had been present at the execution of Gorsas, the first Girondin deputy to mount the scaffold. I, for one, should like to believe that this was true and that William risked his life in October 1793 in order to rejoin Annette, but there is no confirmation of the story. If he went he would have gone in disguise and surely the adventure would have left its mark on his work. Wish-fulfilment may have played its part in this story of his old age.

In an unhappy frame of mind Wordsworth spent some time in London in January 1792 and it is supposed picked up a pittance from newspaper work. He describes himself at this time as "A poet only to myself, to men unknown." It sickened him to watch the preparations in England, his own England, to make war on Liberty, but it comforted him to know that the British army was small and ill-equipped and that the neglect of the years could not be repaired in a day.

When in March the French were defeated at Neerwinden, Wordsworth mourned, mourned over the British victory as later he rejoiced, in company with "all ingenuous youths," when failure set in for British arms. He confesses in *The Prelude* as "truth most painful to record" that he had

> Exulted in the triumph of his soul
> When Englishmen in thousands were o'erthrown
> Left without glory on the field, or driven,
> Brave hearts, to shameful flight.

All out of sympathy with the life around him, he went to see soldiers training on Salisbury Plain and the fleet anchored at Spithead. From the Isle of Wight he writes despondently:

> The American War was still fresh in memory. The struggle which was beginning and which many thought would be brought to a speedy close by the irresistible arms of Great Britain being added to those of the allies, I was assured in my own mind it would be of long continuance and productive of distress and misery beyond all possible calculation. The conviction was pressed upon me by having been a witness during a long residence in Revolutionary France of the spirit which prevailed in that country.

When the British Government suspended the Habeas

Corpus Act in order to be free to deal with those Republican sympathizers who called themselves pro-French, Wordsworth declared that it was acting in a manner to undermine Justice and make an end of Liberty:

> Much have they to account for, who could tear
> By violence, at one decisive rent
> From the best youth in England their dear pride,
> Their joy in England.

By May 1792 he was so desperate as to consider taking Holy Orders in winter or in spring, a step unjustified by his convictions. A Republican at heart he drew some satisfaction from attacking the Bishop of Llandaff for his sermon on "The Wisdom and Goodness of God in having made both Rich and Poor." Both theme and treatment made William's gorge rise. He made it plain that pity for the death of Louis XVI was in his eyes both irrational and weak and that occasions sometimes arise when political virtues must be developed at the expense of moral virtues. He now believed that everything originating in Monarchy was evil and that that which flows from it—inequality, arbitrary distinctions of titles, stars, ribbons, badges, were an outrage on human nature. This attack on the Establishment could not have recommended him to ecclesiastical patrons.

Just when the future appeared most dark William was summoned to the bedside of his Cambridge friend, Raisley Calvert, at Penrith. Calvert was dying of tuberculosis and William stayed with him till the end. He then found that a sum of £900 had been left to him by his friend, who, confident that Wordsworth had "powers and attainments which might be of use to mankind," wished to help him to realize them. The money solved all immediate problems and enabled the poet to settle with Dorothy at Racedown near Crewkerne.

From now on development was sure, for the bequest enabled William and Dorothy to live care-free for seven years in a house lent them by the Pinneys, their Bristol friends. It was while visiting his publisher friend Joseph Cottle at Bristol in 1795 that Wordsworth first met Coleridge. They met occasionally during 1796 and in 1797, in order to be close to him, the Wordsworths transferred from Racedown to Alfoxden. Working together the two poets achieved the most important innovation in English prosody, the publication of *Lyrical Ballads*.

The fact that William was under Home Office observation as a possible spy and a known sympathizer with the Jacobins made it impossible for them to renew their lease of Alfoxden after Lady Day 1798, and this was the spur that drove them abroad. From now on it becomes clearer and clearer that Dorothy was William's real prop and comfort and that no woman except Dorothy was ever again to be able to help Wordsworth in a spiritual sense. Never was he to find another person with whom to share the deeper currents of his life.

*   *   *   *   *

The scene now shifts to Calais. It is 1802, the year of the peace of Amiens. For some weeks English

people have been rushing over to France. William
and Dorothy are among them. Annette is thirty-two
years old and Caroline nearly ten. The Vallons and
the Wordsworths spend day after summer day in close
companionship. What do they find to say to each
other? and what language do they speak? What little
we know about the way they spent their time we glean
from Dorothy, who, though the weather was hot,
managed to catch a chill and could not bathe with the
others. She walked along the sands at low tide and
watched the reflections in the water "more beautiful
than the sky itself, purple waves brighter than precious
stones for ever melting upon the sands." In between
the bathes and the walks they discussed the future
and education of Caroline. Might the Wordsworths
be permitted to adopt her? would Mademoiselle Vallon
consider that possibility? Mademoiselle Vallon sum-
marily dismissed the idea, she adored the child and
could not be parted from her. William must think of
another plan if he wished to keep in touch with her.
In the end the excursion turned out an ordinary seaside
outing for all of them: and it changed nothing, though
it set Dorothy's conscience completely at rest. A
commonplace parting concluded the visit. William
and Dorothy were seen off on the boat from Calais and
Annette and Caroline then made their way back to their
home at Blois. On the whole, as an experience, it had
been unexpectedly flat, but at the same time enormously liberating, for Wordsworth was himself again.
The joy of treading English turf on Dover cliff with
his sister, his "dear companion at his side," made

up for every deficiency in emotional reactions in France.

The experience had taught Dorothy a great deal. She had infused the dead romance with her own imagined ardour and to find the story meant just nothing to either of the principals made her see with quite terrifying clarity just how responsible and important was the rôle she must henceforth play in her brother's life. Her eyes and her heart must in future be dedicated to him. Neither Mary Hutchinson nor any other woman could take her place. Always must she stand fast, always must she be there, for she alone could give her paragon the exact help his genius needed.

Back in England, William showed no haste to rejoin Mary, and no wonder, for the moment of imaginative energy had returned and he was writing more easily than he had written for years. "Milton hadst thou been living in this hour" and four other perfect sonnets came to him at this time. Happy with Dorothy and his two brothers, John and Christopher, he let the days go by. Charles Lamb insisted on their all paying a visit to Bartelemy Fair and, forgiven at last, he was bidden by Canon Cookson to Windsor for a reconciliatory interview. "Riding from Windsor in a long-bodied coach with 12 passengers," Dorothy caught a violent cold and was exceedingly unwell. As soon as she was better, brother and sister posted north to Brompton, where they arrived on the 24th of September after a nine weeks' absence. Mary, looking fat and beaming, greeted them in the avenue; Tom, who was forking corn, waved to them from a waggon. The garden bloomed with autumnal asters and parti-coloured sweet-peas.

Dorothy from her window that evening looked down the avenue to the church where her beloved William was to be married. It was less than half a mile from the farm and stood terraced above a water-meadow. No one knew with what deep apprehensions Dorothy anticipated the marriage ceremony. Five days before the ordeal she wrote to a friend, "I half dread the concentration of all tender feeling, past, present, and future, which will come upon me on the wedding morning."

On the day of the ceremony Dorothy made no attempt to go to the church. William came to her room to say farewell, then she watched him and the others walk down the avenue. It was a little past eight in the morning. Sara had stayed in the house to prepare the wedding breakfast. For Dorothy the waiting time was a time of extreme tension.

> I kept myself as quiet as I could, but when I saw two men running up the walk, coming to tell me it was over, I could stand it no longer, and threw myself on the bed, where I lay in stillness neither hearing nor seeing anything till Sara came upstairs to me and said, "They are coming." This forced me from the bed where I lay and I moved I know not how, straight forward, faster than my strength could carry me, till I met my beloved William and fell upon his bosom. He and John Hutchinson led me to the house and there I stayed to welcome my dear Mary.

When breakfast was over the honeymoon party of three, husband, wife and sister, drove off to the Hambleton hills. Again the Wordsworths arrived at the

Black Swan at Helmsley and warmed themselves at the kitchen hearth. Dorothy dragged William off to see the remains of the castle and then "as dear Mary had never seen a ruined Abbey before except Whitby," she hurried bride and bridegroom downhill to examine Rievaulx.

The trio travelled far and fast on the wedding day, pushing on in the afternoon from Helmsley to Thirsk, and then from Thirsk to Leeming Bar, which they reached at midnight. A very early start next day brought them by luncheon-time to Leyburn. On the road to Hawes one of the horses of their post-chaise becoming restive, they were brought to a standstill in the Ure valley opposite Bolton Castle. There, as a severe storm prevented their getting out, they sat for a while cooped up in the carriage. With her mind's eye fixed on Bolton's most famous prisoner Dorothy exclaimed, "Hard was thy durance poor Queen Mary compared with ours!" which roused William to write a sonnet, "On this our imprisonment," lines subsequently deemed "unworthy of preservation." By Wensleydale the party then drove on to Hawes, where another night was spent, and on Wednesday evening the 6th of October their final destination, the cottage at Town-end, was reached. Unheeding of Mary, William and Dorothy rushed into the steep little garden to inspect their cherished Portugal laurels by candlelight.

ROBERT SURTEES OF MAINSFORTH

ROBERT SURTEES OF MAINSFORTH
(1779–1834)

O NE is so prone to talk of the time in which we live
as mechanized that it is startling to find Carlyle in
1829 characterizing his own day by "the single epithet,
he mechanical age." Four years earlier the first of the
railways, the Stockton-Darlington line, had been opened,
and sportsmen were horrified to see passengers in horse-
drawn coaches glide slowly through the best of Lord
Darlington's hunting country. At once masters of
fox-hounds began to bewail the coming extinction of
field sports. Among those who stood to watch the
grinding collision between new and old world was
Robert Surtees of Mainsforth, whose home, an island
site in an implacable waste of coalfields, now stands a
monument to that collision. The heart of Robert
Surtees was buried in the past, for he was an antiquarian
born and his life-work, *The History of the County of Durham*, is a record as important in its way as Dugdale's
History of the County of Warwick written more than a
century earlier. When asked by a sporting neighbour
why he spent time and money in ferreting out records,
the Squire of Mainsforth retorted, "I wonder why you
spend so much time and money in following a pack of
hounds after a poor hare."

Except for interludes at Oxford and the Inner Temple, Robert Surtees spent his life in Durham and for

Durham. He was born at Mainsforth many years after his parents' marriage and for this reason, if for no other, was like another Durham child, Annabella Milbanke, specially cherished. Brought up like the heiress of the Milbankes, without companions of his own age, he early in life became a self-sufficient little numismatist and acquirer of classical and mediæval lore. When taken to York by his parents he would poke about Micklegate Bar seeking for ancient coins and pay wondering, almost fearful, visits to the grave of the Roman princess under the undertaker's shop on the Knavesmire Road, that up till quite recently might be seen by those in the know.

Educated a few miles from home at Keyper Grammar School, Houghton-le-Spring, the boy there learnt to reverence a rector of former days who had left his mark on the religious education meted out to pupils. This rector, Sir George Wheler, a doctor of Divinity, traveller and collector of manuscripts and "marbles," wrote a treatise on Christian economics entitled *The Protestant Monastery*, and it was in accordance with the teaching of this book that Robert Surtees conducted his life. Though very difficult to come by, the treatise may be read at the British Museum, and in turning its pages we see how much in favour was Sir George of "monasteries for women," for by such means might be solved "the problem of superfluous daughters" and the "taking of them off their wearied parents' hands." The personal discipline advocated in this manual for men and maidens alike involved the keeping of the canonical hours during the day and four watches by night.

In palliation of the title he had given his book Sir George wrote:

> If the name of Monastery be offensive to any as a Popish name, I doubt not but it may be as innocently used to distinguish it from the Romans as the word Church or Faith may be in the like distinction of Popish or Protestant.

There are hymns in the book to "suit a Christian Labourers Practice in the Cornfields, Meadows, and Woods; that whilst he hears the birds and every creature praising their Maker, he might not be silent either in heart or voice." The verses are dedicated to "that mistress of charming conversation" the wife of Lord Crewe, the handsome Bishop of Durham who at Dover Castle had united the trembling child Mary of Modena to the elderly Duke of York. Of the Bishop's wife Sir George Wheler writes panegyrically:

> I must in many a vision describe your Ladyship, at the Altar in most Devout raptures; in your Closet in most ardent Applications; I must show your Ladyship in many a pious Domestick and Publick scene. At Auckland crowded with Poor, Wounded, Sick, Lame and Diseased Neighbours dispensing cures to each of them and everywhere at Durham my Lord's High Almoner.

Primed early in life with a definite and gentlemanly form of religious observance, Robert Surtees adhered rigidly to his creed, saying the *De Profundis* by night and repeating praises, collects, and psalms by day. Each morning on rising he renounced the devil and all his works and read a passage from the Greek Testament. Undeflected from his prescribed course by life at Christchurch or by reading for the Bar in London,

at twenty-three he inherited Mainsforth, settled in
there and after four years of bachelordom took to himself a wife. A delicate and profoundly contented man
from henceforth could say "God has placed me in
Paradise."

Whenever weather and health permitted, he drove
about the country in a gig investigating ruins and
records. His groom called it "weary work, for the
master always stopped the gig, we never could get past
an old building." His friends say that he never sat
down to write doggedly at his History, but would pace
the wide gravel walk at the back of his house and having
well considered his subject would come into the library
and scribble down the result, often in hieroglyphs that
no one but himself could read. By using his accurate
and retentive memory he was able to fit odd pieces of
information together as cubes are fitted into a mosaic.
Aiming at concision, he used as few words as were
compatible with exact statement. Pedigrees, charters,
details of tenure, such as ox-gangs and service of cumin,
inscriptions on monuments, lists of rectors, of mayors,
descriptions of churches, houses, ruins, peculiarities of
tillage and soil, down to the de-pasturing of bees, all
were included in his survey. Fragments that time had
scattered found their place of re-assembly in his mind.
After examining the ruins of Neasham Abbey, he
methodically followed up clues that led to the discovery
of a cross in a garden at Low Middleton, to a Baron of
Greystoke effigy in a private house at Hurworth, to a
wall on Neasham hill crest into which a piece of sculp-
tured stone had been mortared, and inventoried these

items as part and parcel of the Benedictine church. And what he did for one place he did for all, sparing himself no pains if he could achieve a more inclusive accuracy.

Careful as Surtees was to list and describe ancient buildings, he dismisses the modern seats of country gentlemen as unworthy of detailed consideration. Wynyard is economically dealt with as

> one of the most handsome and convenient mansions in the district. It stands without much advantage of prospect, surrounded by a country of deep clay; a fine piece of water stretches along the valley, edged with wood and lawn; there are some pleasing sheltered wood-walks; a handsome bridge crosses the head of the water, and forms the chief approach.

It is not on topography of this sort that Robert Surtees expanded himself or allowed his fancy to play, but on the links with a romantic or tragic past, and the sight of decaying Spanish chestnut trees at Sockburn had the power of evoking in him visions of the vanished world in which he found his true being.

*   *   *   *   *

In youth he had taught himself to write early and mediæval English and had practised the making or faking of antique documents and the composing of old Ballads. The uses he put these attainments to betray a whimsical sense of humour. Everyone knows how neatly he caught Sir Walter Scott in his antiquarian trap, how with great solemnity he despatched to the

Editor of *Minstrelsy of the Scottish Border* ballads of his own contriving, which he alleged had been gathered from "an old body" at Alston Moor. *The Death of Featherstonhaugh*, one of his contrivances, is a masterpiece of likeliness and liveliness. Complete with glossary of archaic terms and historical notes, it reached the delighted Scott, who, entertaining no doubt as to its authenticity, fitted part of it into the first canto of *Marmion*, and later published the whole of it in a revised edition of his *Minstrelsy*. Thanking Surtees warmly for his helpful and numerous letters, Scott went so far as to tell him that he has been "chiefly the cause" of his writing *Marmion* at all, and in February 1808 when the poem was published he sent a note to Mainsforth saying: "I have to request your acceptance of a thumping quarto entitled *Marmion*, in which you will find I have availed myself with suitable acknowledgments of the Ballad of the Feud between the Ridleys and Featherstonhaugh family."

Sure enough, Surtees on opening the book read of "a Northern harper rude" entertaining Lord Marmion in Edinburgh with "a rhyme of deadly feud."

> How the fierce Ridleys and Thirlwalls all
> Stout Willemoteswick,
> And hard riding Dick,
> And Hughie of Hawdon and Will of the Wall
> Have set on Sir Albany Featherstonhaugh
> And taken his life at the Deadman's Shaw.

With the Ballads, Surtees had enclosed a Latin note purporting to have been written by a monk of Durham in the margin of a copy of Burthogg's book *On the*

Nature of Spirits.   It may be from this note that Lord Marmion's encounter with the Elfin knight was derived.

Scott made, as he says, suitable acknowledgments as to the source of his Ridley-Featherstonhaugh rhymes in the amended edition of *Minstrelsy of the Scottish Border*.

> This old Northumbrian ballad was taken down from the recitation of a woman of eighty years of age, mother of one of the miners of Alston Moor, by an agent for the lead mines there, who communicated it to my friend and correspondent R. Surtees Esquire of Mainsforth.   She said she had not heard it for many years; but when she was a girl it used to be sung at the merry makings "till the roof rung again."

Another well-appreciated contribution to Scott's collection of Border Ballads was *Bartram's Dirge* with its jaunty lines.

> They shot him dead on the Ninestone Rigg
> Beside the headless cross,
> And they left him lying in his blood
> Under the moor and moss.

Surtees purported to have acquired the *Dirge* from "the imperfect recitation of a withered crone Anne Douglas who weeded in my garden."   Scott, in acknowledging it, called it "the most beautiful fragment I have seen this many a day."   A Mainsforth neighbour, Mr. Raine, less gullible than Scott, wrote against this ballad in his copy of Minstrelsy, *aut Rob*, *aut Diab*, to which Surtees later on added the words *Ita*, *teste seipso*.

Not content with supplying Scott with new material,

153

Surtees kept on urging him to take up "the interesting periods of '15 and '45." Why, he asked, should poor posterity trace these thrilling days only in the cold pages of a professed historian? Did not Scotland boast of a Minstrel?

> Should you ever be induced to such a continuation of your poetical labours and collections, I think I can promise you "Lord Derwentwater's Good night"—the only Englishman whose fate is inwoven with most of your countrymen in '15.

It is not beyond rational surmise that the impulsion communicated by Surtees to Scott in this way may have resulted in the drafting of *Waverley*. Scott replies:

> Certainly I will not renounce the idea of doing something to preserve these stories and the memory of the times and manners . . . your kind encouragement confirms me in the resolution that something I must do and speedily. . . .

In due course *Lord Derwentwater's Good night* reached Scott.

> No more along the banks of Tyne
> I'll rove in autumn gray,
> No more I'll hear at early dawn
> The laverocks wake the day.
> Farewell, farewell, George Collingwood,
> Since fate has put us down,
> If thou and I have lost our lives
> King James has lost his crown.

This time the medium of communication had been a child. "The Ballad," wrote Surtees,

> is in such state as I could procure it. This latter, notwithstanding two or three collations from recitation, still appears

evidently imperfect and I have never met with it in print. Some of the stanzas at the end are so inferior in elegance, and even so defective in grammar, that one would scarce suppose them from the same hand, even allowing for the usual corruptions *in ore vulgi.* I have pieced it together for you as well as I can, and it is, after all, much the best thing I have met with on the subject. The copy enclosed is by a little girl here, who was taught it by a servant, and remembers more of it than anyone else. Lord D's request to be buried in Northumberland stands on historical evidence; but the fear of popular tumult prevented its being complied with and I think he was buried in St. Giles Churchyard, Holborn. You will recollect Lord Lovat's wish to have all the old women in Scotland howl at his obsequies. Lord D's milder genius may be supposed to have sighed for the more elegant offering of a wreath of flowers for the maids of Tyndale. I may further mention that Lady D. used all her influence to engage her husband in the Jacobite cause.

From time to time Surtees would furnish Scott with items of arresting information supposed to have been extracted from parish registers or other ancient documents. For instance, in August 1807 he writes:

As I have nothing else to send you I shall give you the dimensions of an immense snake which I stumbled on in the said register, in searching for other matters.

1569 November Memorand. That a certine Italian brought into the cittee of Doresme Ye 11th of June in Ye yeare aforesayd, a very greate, strange, and monstrous serpent, in length sixteene feete, in quantitie and dimensions greeter than a greate horse, which same was taken and killed by speciall Policies in Ethiopia, within the Turks dominions. But before it was killed it had devoured (as is creditably thought) more than a thousande persons and also destroied a wholle contrey.[1]

What Scott's reaction to this excerpt was we do not know. It was followed up by a legendary fragment to the effect that "Julius Cæsar founded the parish church of Chillingham." "We should," wrote Surtees, "have been quite in the dark about this were it not for a nameless priest of Durham," who recorded,

> How Jules Cæsar, Roman Emperour, prikked in conscience for the murder of Mark Antiny, builded ye Paroche Churche of Shillyngham.

To this suspect communication Scott replied blandly:

> The luminous notices of the foundation of the church at Chillingham serve to correct many errors vulgarly entertained concerning ancient history. I wish it had been more particular in the murder of Mark Antony which has been shockingly misrepresented by contemporary historians [March 4, 1809].

Surtees next draws Scott's attention to a ballad coincident with the Rising of the North—*The Ryde of Rookhope*. He comments on the history and significance of the allusions contained in it and as usual Scott expressed gratitude for "repeated favours." There is a quite enchanting and solemn waggishness about Surtees as a pedagogue, and never is he in appearance more demure than when he is pulling Scott's leg. He even questions him as to the origin of certain of the words and phrases that appear in the spurious ballads. What

---

[1] See Appendices, *County of Durham*, Vol. IV.

are "habs," he enquires, and is not "married *upon* a Willoughby" a Scotch mode of expression?

Scott worshippers today like to assume that the two authors had a good laugh over the fakes produced by Surtees, but I do not believe this can be true, as in 1830 Scott, when writing a New Introduction to his *Minstrelsy*, retained the Featherstonhaugh Ballad with acknowledgment to Mr. Surtees and commendation of his "learned proofs" of its authenticity.

* * * * *

When Mr. and Mrs. Walter Scott drove down from Edinburgh on their first and only visit to Mainsforth in April 1809, the countryside round Ferryhill was undulating, rural and green. The Hall on the hill, now shrouded from view by trees, was then visible from a distance. Possibly then, as now, coal outcropped in the woods, and from the rolled gravel paths of the garden black sand may have oozed after rain. The Hall cannot have changed much in the last hundred years. It is a four-square, three-storied building, to which additions have been tacked. A comfortable house, reconstructed internally at differing dates, it contains some rooms that are old, panelled, and allegedly haunted, and others furnished in a reassuringly Victorian way. On the ground floor is a small library containing, among other books, first editions of Scott's works presented by the author and inscribed to "Richard" Surtees, for somehow in the beginning of their acquaintance Scott had got it into his head that his benefactor's name was not Robert but Richard, and Richard it remained for him. When Mrs. Surtees suggested that Scott should be corrected Surtees said "it is not worth while to put him right."

From the bedroom occupied by Mr. and Mrs. Scott during their visit to Mainsforth issued a slip-room wherein, according to family tradition, Scott wrote part of *The Antiquary*. I recognized it at once as just the kind of place Scott would have chosen to write in—a sort of indoor niche overlooking the garden, like the outdoor niche overlooking the Greta where his long poem *Rokeby* was written—but I was obliged to discount the validity of the legend, as Scott stayed but once at Mainsforth, breaking his journey for one night or perhaps two on his way to London and even though a quick worker, in forty-eight hours he could have accomplished little. Before leaving the Hall, the newly-laurelled author of *Marmion* planted an oak tree on the lawn. It is now browning at the extremities from disapproval of its situation, feet in a coal seam, head in carbonized air.

By many people Surtees is thought of merely as one of Scott's numerous friends. It was Scott in *Harold the Dauntless* who advertised the affection existing between them. The third canto of the poem opens with an address to Durham Cathedral, in which he expresses envy of "my Surtees happier lot" in living amidst the imposing relics of mediævalism, rather than in Edinburgh, but apart from his overshadowing friendship with Scott, Robert Surtees, however, had a very complete existence of his own. The closely printed folio volumes of *The History of the County of Durham* that were published in 1816, 1820, and 1823 are all impressive witness to the steady industry, the wit and the varied acquirement of the squire of Mainsforth. The fourth and last volume came out long after his death.

Though grateful to Surtees for all the help he had given him, Scott was never quite at his ease with him. There was, it may be imagined, something strict, particular and critical about the squire of Mainsforth which made genial, jolly intercourse impossible. An inkling of this is to be found in a letter from Scott to Robert Southey: "If you make any stay in Durham, let me know as I wish you to know my friend Surtees of Mainsforth. He is an excellent antiquary, some of the rust of which study has clung to his manners: but he is good-hearted." In other words, Southey is given to understand that the antiquary is not so crabbed as at first sight might appear, and that his creakiness wears off in intercourse. It is unlikely that a man leading Surtees's almost cloistered life could ever be familiar with a man so expansive as Walter Scott. Perhaps he was never very familiar with anyone. He was stand-offish enough on paper with the wife to whom he was devoted, signing himself "sincerely" or at best "very sincerely." Unlike Scott his life did not cause him to rub elbows with strangers or greet friends daily in an Advocates' court. To some extent he may be said to have had the fastidious tastes of a recluse, for being a delicate man the harsh Durham winter obliged him to spend many days in his library. Though he could in no way compete with shooting and fox-hunting neighbours or indeed share their pleasures, he did his duty as a squire, for when hounds met at Mainsforth he provided a hunt breakfast and sometimes, if the meet was early, accommodation on the previous night for hounds, hunt servants, and master.

Always as the background of his life and its chief concern loomed the monumental History of Durham. To compile it, he quartered the country in summer, and pored over archives in winter. It was an absorbing occupation and compensated him for being half an invalid. Like many half-invalids he was a gardener and derived deep enjoyment from the delayed savour of a northern spring. When riding alone through lanes and woods he scattered seeds of every shade of columbine. He also raised stonecrop and pinks upon his garden wall so that passers-by might benefit, and I think he had in himself the courage and patience of flowers.

Like Scott, Surtees had a great affection for dogs, and at breakfast was surrounded by greyhounds and pointers. He could not bear to pain animals and would not destroy old ponies or even so much as a wasps' nest. For a particularly dear dog, Carlo, he wrote an epitaph which A. E. Housman might have composed for a dog of his own.

> Green Erin gave him gentle birth
> O'er lilied France in youth he stray'd
> Four summer suns; in English earth
> He sleeps beneath the walnut shade.

Surtees knew every dog in Durham and always greeted

them, for he said man was the deity of the dog and must show benevolence.

His friends said that his devoted attachment to the secluded domesticity of Mainsforth was the motive for his declining the offers that were from time to time made to him of a seat in Parliament and of a prebendal stall in Durham, which Bishop Barrington had promised him if he would take Holy Orders. But to the end he preferred his private labours to any public post.

When a bill was brought before Parliament for a projected railway through his property it was strenuously opposed at his instance by friends in both Houses of Parliament. The scheme was alleged to be of public advantage and a peer who was supporting the Bill said to him, "Surtees, is there no other place upon which you could set your heart? If there be we have perfect confidence in your honour, name your price for Mainsforth and you shall have it without another word." No hesitation delayed Surtees's reply: "My Lord, buy me Blenheim."

At the end of January 1834 Surtees caught a severe cold on the outside of a coach returning home from Sunderland, pleurisy developed with pain and gradual lessening of resistance. Looking round his library on one of his last days, he said to his wife, "Annie, I shall never be here again, these books will be yours." "So may they, Surtees, and I should never like to part with them; but don't you think it would be well to send your manuscripts to some public library where they would be of use?" Surtees replied, "You are right, and if it should please God that I should live a day or two, I will make a selection of them myself."

It was his fate to die at the close of a long dark winter. One sunny morning, he sighed and said, "I shall never see the peach-blossoms or the flowers of spring," and went on to murmur his dear John Leyden's lines,

> But sad is he that dies in spring
> When flowers begin to blow and larks to sing
> And makes it doubly hard with life to part.

A few days later, he said to his wife, "Annie, I am very ill, I would have liked to receive the Sacrament, but I am too ill now to send for anyone, but I give it to myself. Don't make yourself uneasy as to my state. I think as deeply as man can think. . . . I have left you for your life every sixpence I possess and I hope the sun will go down brightly shining on your latter days. But let us talk no more of the affairs of this world."

He was lying by his own request alone and in darkness while Mrs. Surtees watched in the next room. Hearing a single stroke of a chiming clock he rapped for his medicine. His wife entered saying, "Surtees, it is not one, yet." "Yes, it is," he replied, and she contradicting him said, "You are mistaken, it cannot be."— "Nay then," he said chidingly, "Annie, what is to become of the world if you are beginning to lie!" Next day he said, "Annie, I am dead," and the answer he heard was a prayer that he might sleep in Jesus.

Austere in life, austere in death, Surtees's coffin was borne by men from his estate to its deep grave in the limestone rock at Bishop Middleham.   Southey, who was present as a mourner, describes the funeral.

Though it is more in accordance with the natural rhythm of nature to die in the autumn than the spring, Surtees's deep regret at quitting the life he loved may have been tempered with a melancholy satisfaction in knowing that he was leaving behind him an imperishable record of the county he adored.

ROKEBY AND SIR WALTER SCOTT

ROKEBY AND SIR WALTER SCOTT

Rokeby, a demesne curiously situated on a tongue of land between two rivers, is just outside the county of Durham on the Yorkshire bank of the Tees. I was eager to see the place because of Scott's long topographical poem describing the place and the district round it. Scott had succumbed instantaneously to the pervasive charm of Rokeby; my capitulation was also immediate. No place more overpoweringly conveys the flavour and sentiment of days that can never return. To begin, as I did, to explore the policies on a sunny morning in June is to experience to the full the sensation of having been plunged deep into the late eighteenth century. Yews of great age and size border the Greta and give the intruder a feeling of horror and of gloom. The huge fir-tree boles that here and there pierce the overhead canopy of sable, serve to accent the dismal character of the woods. Except for a rushing stream there is no noise: yew needles effectively muffle all footfalls and one starts apprehensively as one stumbles on a headstone, half expecting to meet the Dobie or female spectre that is said to haunt the adjacent tower of Mortham.

Nothing, I think, has changed more in English people than their feeling for the sun. The men and women of Georgian England differ sharply from us in this respect. The Rousseau influence from France and the gothic miasma from Germany impregnated society with results that may still be discerned in a few places. Rokeby is one of them for fortunately it has not been improved or indeed very much disturbed during the last century of so-called progress.

The pleasure garden of the early nineteenth century was no mere flower-border or alpine lay-out; it was a grassed enclosure of varying proportions, mossy, moist, and sheltered by evergreen trees and shrubs. Ilex, holly, box, and laurel planted in clusters by gravelled paths formed tunnels of greenery round the house. Wordsworth's ideal garden was a green one and to the romantic heart of Scott ravines "impervious to the sun" were asylums fostering imagination. And it was not eminent people only who developed a predilection for cloistering themselves in dark shrubberies: every country house was furnished as a matter of course with these appurtenances. Every suburban villa went in for them too. They had their practical uses in the masking of outdoor lavatories and backdoor entrances. That patron of the arts, Sir George Beaumont, when building Coleorton to the design of Sir Nathaniel Dance, implored the greatest poet of the age to plan a garden in which it would be possible to meditate in seclusion while listening to the drip of water. The very cult of cascades that is so noticeable in letters and memoirs of the period, and which is specially accented by Dorothy Wordsworth and Jane Austen, conveyed, it is evident, a thrill of sublimity to every educated mind. Today, no one wants to wander in the shade, and no one wishes to build rustic refuges in woods, for sun-seeking and sun-bathing have taken the place of the older liking for coolness and shade. It may be that the change came in with sun-pictures when it was suddenly realized what magic quality resided in its beams, or it is possible that a changing taste in beverages and clothes have had their effect on manners, for it is unlikely that men drinking their nightly bottle of port and wearing beaver hats, broadcloth coats and voluminous neckcloths, would care to expose their overheated bodies to the direct rays of the sun. Port indeed may have been one of the principal factors inducing gentlemen to take delight in pacing the well-kept paths of their policies and in constructing gothic shelters from which to contemplate vistas of evergreens conducting the eye till it came to rest on some stone urn or leaden effigy. The argument may appear to break down when we look at the ladies in their muslin gowns and satin slippers, but it was a man's world they had to fit into, and anyway, most of their life was spent indoors.

Many years ago I stayed at a house in Ireland from which walks extended along the high cliffs of the Suir, walks punctuated by little summer-houses each furnished with elegant chairs of rural design, tea-sets of unglazed Wedgwood, and bookshelves on which stood duodecimos of Rousseau's novels, Thomson's Seasons, and Cowper's poems. These evidences of genteel culture were destroyed long since in the civil wars, but they conveyed to me a sense of elegance, of a delicate enjoyment of life that can never be resuscitated.

*   *   *   *   *

On his first visit to Rokeby, which he found his host calling Rookby, Scott was stimulated to write, for ready to his eye was the perfect setting for romantic tragedy. Surely Rokeby was the most enviable place a man could live in. Not only was the rocky course of Greta reminiscent of his beloved Roslin Glen and his courting days by Irthling, but over and above these charms it boasted in the face of the cliff a little cave shaded by trees which, if furnished with a table, would serve him as an open-air study wherein might be composed his next rhyming narrative. So inspiring a spot must induce a flood of verse. In 1809 Scott was known exclusively as a writer of verse. It was not till five years later that he published his first novel. Bubbling over with enthusiasm, he enquired whether Rokeby was virgin soil or whether other rhymers had preceded him in the field. Surely verses must exist concerning the place and its legends? A ballad Surtees of Mainsforth had furnished him with, *The Raid of Rookhope*, might perhaps prove to be the story of Rokeby in disguise, but the ballad merely dealt with Weardale and he had to fall back on inventing a tale of the Civil War which should include adventures in the enchanted grounds he was now discovering. Finding that the Barons of Rokeby had lost their lands in championing King Charles I, Scott chose the days following the battle of Marston Moor (July 3, 1644) as the period for his poem, for he felt that the confusion ensuing after the fight would lend itself to almost any adventure or circumstance. His story must be called *Rokeby* and Barnard Castle must be included in its scope.

Under the Commonwealth, the Lords of Rokeby had been replaced by a family called Robinson, and it was from them that Morritt's father had acquired the estate. Scott's links with early friends were always based on similarity of taste and interest: the owner of Rokeby was no exception. He was an antiquary and collector of ballads. When he first introduced himself to Scott by sending him a drawing of Bishop Bell's tomb in Carlisle Cathedral, he quickly followed it up by offering him a ballad of his own composing, *The Curse of Moy*, for inclusion in the third volume of *Minstrelsy of the Border*, the volume containing modern ballads. As a young man Morritt had travelled in Greece and had visited the Troad to confute Bryant's hypothesis that Troy town was not taken by the Greeks. He knew Italian well and had made translations from Metastasio. In short, he was a rich and scholarly man with taste so good as to buy the Rokeby Venus, and sense so good as to help found the Travellers' Club. Given a letter of introduction to Scott by their mutual friend Lady Louisa Stuart, he halted on his way through Edinburgh in July 1808 in order to be shown the local sights by the already famous author of *Marmion*. Walter Scott was at this time enjoying life and fame to the full. In the Raeburn portrait painted this year we see a solidly built young man sitting on stone steps beside a ruin. Camp, his favourite dog, is by his side. Camp is growing old but his master is full of vigour and only beginning to realize what literary prizes lie within his grasp. Delighted on the occasion of Morritt's visit to show his guest Roslin and Hawthornden,

they spent a whole day together by the Esk. The ray
of Scott's own romance with the little French girl still
illuminated Lasswade, and the *cottage orné* was tenderly
shown off, for the low house with its beehive thatch was
to him the symbol of early rapture. Morritt recalled
for Lockhart's benefit the way Scott had talked about
the place, the jasmine bush by the porch, the willows
he and Charlotte had twined into an arch, the table
they had made, the honeysuckle bower, the arm-linked
walks by moonlight. "To be sure it is not much of a
lion to show a stranger," he said to Morritt, but after
all he had been happy there, and it revived old joys to
exhibit the place even to a new acquaintance.

The meeting of the two authors was such a success
that it was decided that on their way home from Braham
the Morritts should stay at Ashestiel, the Scotts' Tweed-
side home. It was a fine opportunity for Scott to introduce them to "the wonders of Yarrow and the beauties
of Ettricke," and nothing on this occasion impressed
Morritt more than Scott's easy friendly intercourse
with all classes of neighbours. Scott on his side was
pleased with Morritt, and wrote to Joanna Baillie that
his new friend's erudition was not of an "overbearing
kind, which was lucky for him, as his own classical
equipment was slender," and that "for a man of the
world his nature was unimpaired."

In April 1809 Mr. and Mrs. Scott made "a rapid
and fatiguing journey to Half Moon Street" on business connected with the Commission then sitting in
London on Scotch Law. While in London Scott
busied himself in helping Murray, Ellis, and Gifford to

organize the new *Quarterly Review* which was being set up in the Tory interest as a rival to the *Edinburgh Review*. As soon as possible, Scott rushed round to see the Morritts at their house in Portland Place. There he was made a great fuss of and soon became the lion of their evening parties. As *Marmion* had been read by everyone, and Scott personally unknown to society, he was immensely run after. This, up to a point he enjoyed, but he confided to Mrs. Clephane that though always willing to oblige Morritt by appearing in his drawing-room, he got "a little tired of being a tee-to-tum." Scott's behaviour at Morritt's parties seems according to his host to have been most ingratiating. He would say on being told to show off his tricks:

> All this is very flattering and civil, and if people are amused with hearing me tell a parcel of old stories, or recite a pack of ballads to lovely young girls or gaping matrons, they are easily pleased, and a man would be very ill natured who would not give pleasure so cheaply conferred.

Morritt records that, when Scott arrived to dine with him, he would look round the room and, if he saw any new faces, would say to his host, "Well, do you want me to play the lion to-day? I will roar, if you like, to your heart's content." As soon as the party dispersed he would laugh at himself and say, "Yet know that I one Smug a joiner am no lion fierce." Brown-haired, vigorous, happy Walter Scott radiated good humour and happiness, and whether he was conversing with the Princess of Wales at Blackheath, or talking with demure Joanna Baillie at Hampstead, he managed to entertain all companies and to preserve his modest balance as the countryman in town.

After two busy months in London the Scotts in the middle of June 1809 made their way to Yorkshire. When the London mail set them down at Greta Bridge they found themselves close to the sphinx-ornamented gates of Rokeby Park. The short avenue led to a country house designed as a cube with lesser cubes on either side forming the wings. A low entrance hall on the ground level with Egyptian pillars supporting the roof gave them no hint of the magnificence of the reception-rooms they supported. The large dining-room, with its Adam decoration picked out in scarlet and gold, the saloon with its pictures, made an impression of comfort and grandeur on the visitors, while the actual situation and setting of the house struck Scott as essentially romantic. From the hot sun on the gravel sweep in front of the house he plunged into the shady woods and followed Greta river coursing "o'er sheets of marble grey." It was a never-to-be-forgotten picture. Morning after morning he followed the stream tearing over its limestone floor till it joined the even more vigorous Tees. "The two most beautiful and rapid rivers of the north, Greta and Tees, join current in the demesne," wrote Scott ecstatically to George Ellis. High above the right bank of Greta stood Mortham Tower, and down on Tees bank the lovely Priory of Egleston. To a lover of mediævalism the place was almost too perfect. In company with his host Scott hastened to make himself acquainted with the neighbourhood, with Deepdale and Cat Castle, Cotherston village with the rock rising over the crown of the wood still called Pendragon Castle, and Wycliffe where "the daystar of the Reformation" first rose on England. Winston, Gainford, Scargill, Brignall, and the moors beyond, he scoured them all. Already in his fertile mind verses began to shape themselves, and as he gazed out from Balliol's Tower upon the Tees encircling Barnard Castle the countryside became re-peopled with historic ghosts—Philip of Mortham, Oswald of Wycliffe, Matilda of Rokeby. Every place was suddenly endowed with an owner and a story. Tapestrywise a pseudo-romance of pseudo-chivalry was projected over the landscape. Scott saw, as he gazed out from his rocky cave above the river,

> From his fair hall on Greta Banks
> The Knight of Rokeby lead the ranks
> To aid the valiant Northern Earls
> Who drew the sword for Royal Charles
> Mortham by marriage near allied
> His sister had been Rokeby's bride
> Philip of Mortham raised his band
> And march'd at Fairfax's command
> While Wycliffe bound by many a train
> Of kindred out with wily Vane
> Made Barnard's battlements his shield.

Morritt pointed out to him that it might be advisable to antedate his narrative if he was set on bringing Barnard Castle into the action, since it had not been used as a fortress after the Rising of the North. Indeed Cromwell, the castle being in his day uninhabitable, had been obliged at the time of Marston Moor to occupy lodg-

175

ings.   Surely, argued Morritt, it would be better to set
the story in the time of the Wars of the Roses.   Civil
war for civil war it had two poetical sides, and one cannot say that about the later war, for the Roundheads
though "politically right, were sad materials for poetry.
Even Milton could not make much of them."   Scott
must be careful too to avoid the Rising of the North, as
if he dares abuse Elizabeth he will be accused of being
an abettor of Popery.   Arguments of this sort did not
deflect the author from his purpose: he had chosen his
period and would abide by it.

Verse by this time had become second nature to Scott
and a natural medium of expression, but it is noticeable in *Rokeby* that he was becoming increasingly careless and slapdash in his rhyming.   The facile lines
came pounding along only too fluently as he paced the
banks of Greta, or nibbled his quill pen in the cave.
The writing is almost like that of a letter or a diary.

> But here 'twixt rock and river grew
> A dismal grove of sable yew
> With whose sad tints were mingled seen
> The blighted firs sepulchral green
> Seem'd that the trees their shadows cast
> The earth that nourished them to blast
> For never knew that swarthy grove——

At this point one feels he must have hesitated and then
contented himself with setting down one of the silliest
lines in the poem,

> The verdant hues that fairies love.

As he stood by Mortham Keep he jotted down his plain
impression,

> 'Twas a fair scene, the sunbeam lay
> On battle tower and portal grey;
> And from the grassy slopes he sees
> The Greta flow to meet the Tees.

One song at least must have burbled up out of sheer lightness of heart in lines that sang themselves:

> O, Brignall Banks are wild and fair
> And Greta Woods are green.

Such lyrical outbursts were filed for use when the skeleton of the narrative should have formulated itself in his mind.

The story of *Rokeby* is extremely complicated and shows every sign of having been pieced together out of a dozen anecdotes. Though its action takes only five days we have to learn so much about the previous history of the actors that few people nowadays can be bothered to disentangle its convolutions. When Scott left the Morritts' house he had a budget of verses and notes in his valise and on these he worked at home, but the poem was not so easy to complete. Three cantos written, he submitted one of them to Morritt, who immediately tried to dissuade him from completing the poem on his original and sometimes inaccurate jottings. Having accepted the dedication Morritt felt he had a call on Scott to make the poem as good as he could. After all, it dealt with his own estate and it was always possible that Rokeby in consequence of its publication might become a tourist centre. Had not both Flodden and Loch Katrine been overrun by readers of *Marmion* and the *Lady of the Lake*? Scott demurred to revision and said that the publishers were screaming for copy and that he was pressed for money for Abbotsford. Morritt, however, insisted that he should not scamp his work in deference to any publisher. He must return at once to Rokeby to fill in details of description and geography.

> Do not be persuaded to risk your established fame on this hazardous experiment. If you want a few hundreds . . . I happen at this moment to have five or six for which I have no sort of demand. . . .
>
> Surely it would be worth your while to spend a week of your time and a portion of your Old Man's salary in a mail coach flight hither were it merely to renew your acquaintance with the country, and to rectify the little misconceptions of a cursory view.

And so it came about that on a summer day three years after the first visit Mr. and Mrs. Scott and the children set out for Rokeby. Walter Scott rode a horse, Walter junior a pony, and Mrs. Scott and Sophia drove in a carriage. The children changed mounts during the journey, and everyone was in admirable spirits when the cavalcade reached Flodden, the battle-field Scott had long promised to display and explain to his youngsters. Mamma and the children had soon reason to be proud of Papa and his celebrity, for at the local inn where the carriage horses were baited, the innkeeper began to tell Mr. Scott how greatly *Marmion* had benefited his custom. Out of gratitude he craved permission to alter his sign, which bore painted on it a foaming tankard, to a head of Scott. Smilingly the poet replied that to his mind a foaming tankard was the more attractive and suitable sign, but the man was so persistent that his house must in some way be identified with the maker of his fortune that he insisted Scott should choose him a motto from the well-fingered copy of *Marmion* in his hand. Opening the book at random the author's eye was caught by the black letter inscription,

> Drink, weary pilgrim, drink and pray
> For the kind soul of Sybil Gray,

and he said, "Well, my friend, what more would you have?" and pointed out that if one letter were struck out of the first line it would make an excellent motto for any innkeeper:—

> Drink, weary pilgrim, drink and PAY.

From Flodden the party proceeded to Hexham, a favourite haunt of Scott in youth, and then to Bishop Auckland. While they were applying to be shown the public rooms at Auckland Castle the Bishop recognized Walter Scott, and imposed himself upon the party as its guide. This wholly delightful surprise was the cause of a new friendship. After displaying the great Zubarans of Joseph and his brethren in the dining-room and the portraits in the saloon, Bishop Shute Barrington swept the Scotts off to morning service in the chapel and then made them all breakfast with him. By the time the travellers should have set out for Rokeby, Scott and the Bishop were getting on so famously that they could not be parted. Observing that he "liked to feel his mount under him" the bishop, aged seventy-nine, got on to a curveting horse and accompanied the Scott cavalcade for ten miles of the road to Rokeby.

Before taking leave he made Scott promise that he would halt at Auckland Castle on future journeys to the south.

Next morning at breakfast Scott announced that what he really required for the completion of his poem was "a good robber's cave and an old church of the right sort." Morritt at once ordered the horses and rode out with his guest to the slate quarries of Brignall and the ruined priory of Egleston. The quarry at once became

> . . . the deserted mine . . .
> The banquet hall and fortress too
> Of Denzil and his desperate crew.

Noticing that his companion made lists of all the wild flowers and herbs that grew on the side of the crag near the cave, Morritt could not help chaffing him, saying that violets and primroses would be every bit as poetical as the humble weeds he was examining. Scott replied gravely enough that "in nature no two scenes were exactly alike and that whoever copied truly what was before his eyes would possess the same variety in his descriptions and exhibit an imagination as boundless as the range of nature in the scenes he recorded; where-as whoever trusted to imagination would soon find his mind circumscribed and contracted to a few favourite images and the repetition of these would sooner or later produce that very monotony and barrenness which had always haunted descriptive poetry in any but the patient worshippers of truth. Besides which, local names and peculiarities make a fictitious story look so much better in the face." Morritt wondered about this, his idea of the imaginative faculty being different, but he did notice that Scott seemed to care little about landscape for its own sake, or even ruins unless they were connected with a local legend. His genius seemed to be fired by tradition only. Morritt sometimes could find no story to tell about a building. Scott would laugh and say, "Let us make one, there is nothing so easy to make as tradition."

When he had seen his fill of landscape, ruins and quarries Scott clambered up once more to the shallow recess in the cliff face above Greta and sat down to complete his overdue poem. Placed within the cave for his convenience was a rustic table with a reed surface, at which he wrote the descriptive passages that still are recognizable today. With Mortham keep behind him, Greta sliding from ledge to ledge below him, Rokeby with its trees in front of him, guide-books and maps beside him, he worked with the celerity for which he was famous.

> 'Tis mine to tell an onward tale
> Hurrying as best I can along
> The hearers and the hasty song.

Striving by every means in his power to get actuality and accuracy into his lines, he consulted Hollinshed, Lediard, gazetteers, histories, and road-books. So successful was he in the end that his poem may still serve to re-animate a countryside which no other eye than Scott's has in the poetic sense perceived. Were it not for him, Greta and Tees might have poured out their symphony with no audience than that of the gentry of the Hall, or the people of the village.

Even Morritt was satisfied in the end and declared *Rokeby* to be the best of his friend's poems. This is not the general opinion, but as Lockhart sagely observes:

> The admirable, perhaps unique fidelity of the local descriptions might alone have swayed, for I will not say it perverted, the judgment of the lord of that beautiful and thenceforth classic domain.

This fidelity was painfully achieved: it was not easy to satisfy Morritt and the writer got extremely tired of *Rokeby* before he had done with the poem. At one moment he told Lady Abercorn that he had thrown most of it on the fire, being convinced he had "corrected the spirit out of it, as a lively pupil is sometimes flogged into a dunce by a severe schoolmaster." The Scott family went back to Scotland in July and Scott toiled on at the poem. He was able to submit three cantos of the revised version to Morritt in October 1812, and hard upon them, or conceivably in response to further criticism from Morritt, Scott followed after to make further corrections. Morritt indulged in a rather tiresome jocularity about the way the poem might affect him. He may even be obliged "by the influx of Cockney romancers, artists, illustrators and sentimental tourists" to leave Rokeby, and with a further dig in the ribs, "I shall raise the rent of my inn at Greta Bridge on the first notice of your book as I hear the people at Callander have made a fortune by you."

Scott was not sorry to leave Rokeby: his poem had become a millstone round his neck. At Christmas-

time the author told some of his friends that he felt a
kind of melancholy in concluding a poem with the year,
but this was one of those strange little excursions into
sentiment in which he occasionally indulged. Really,
as he confided to Gillies, he was "sick tired of the grew-
some tale" and had had the greatest difficulty in finishing it. *Rokeby* was published on New Year's Day,
1813, and on January 10th we find the writer happily
announcing, "The book has gone off bobbishly, the
wholesalers have bought it up."

No wonder he was pleased, for it put money at his
disposal to spend on Abbotsford. Life was good and
no suspicion of failure cankered it. Lockhart, however, saw the inherent weakness of his latest production. It was almost unintelligible till one knew the
locality after which it was named, then and only then
could one appreciate its charm. Too much perhaps
had been sacrificed to accuracy.

Booksellers and publishers ordered the first edition
with gusto anticipating for it a success as great as that
achieved by *The Lady of the Lake*. Suddenly to their
surprise there appeared in the *Twopenny Postbag* a skit
too apt and well-deserved not to injure the retail sale
of the poem.

Tom Moore held the romance up to ridicule as a
kind of gazetteer, the first of a series, in which the
country houses of the great should be described in
rhyme.

Should you feel any touch of poetical glow
We've a scheme to suggest . . . Mr. Scott you must know
(Who we're sorry to say now works for the Row)

183

Having quitted the Border to seek new renown
Is coming, by long quarto stages to town
And beginning with Rokeby (the job's sure to pay)
Means to *do* all the gentlemen's seats on the way.
Now the scheme is (though none of our hackneys can beat
    him)
To start a fresh poet through Highgate to meet him;
Who by means of quick profit—no revises—long coaches
May do a few villas before Scott approaches.
Indeed if our Pegasus be not curst shabby
He'll reach without foundering at least Woburn Abbey.

With this totally unexpected attack on *Rokeby* came
to an end Scott's rôle as a poet. He was the first to
realize the old game was up and that it was for him to
find a new opening. Philosophically, he began to
go through the piles of manuscript in his drawers.
Finished and half-finished novels, one of which must
now be reconstructed and launched upon the perilous
ocean of public opinion.

With the amusing bravura that Scott sometimes
affected he said in sending a copy of the poem *Rokeby*
to Joanna Baillie, "I hope you will like Bertram to the
end: he is a Caravaggio sketch which I may acknowledge to you—but tell it not in Gath—I rather pique
myself upon." His women friends admired *Rokeby*
as they had admired all his other poetical romances.
Miss Baillie read it through twice, was moved to tears,
and called it sublime. Lady Abercorn was an enthusiast for it. The Princess of Wales and Lady Charlotte
Bury at Blackheath listened to Tom Campbell reading
it aloud after dinner and thought it very fine indeed.
Harriet Shelley irritated Shelley by reading it to him in

a coach travelling to Edinburgh. Byron ordered it
from Murray with a "Who the devil is Rokeby?"
Morritt also had no doubts about the merits of the
poem and viewed with favourable and indulgent eyes
the romance that contributed to the enhancement and
appreciation of his dear estate. The general public
neither read the poem nor flocked to the scene of the
story, and for this reason Rokeby remains to this hour
the unspoilt resort of quietude, a living monument to
days when sensibility to romantic surroundings was
accounted the acme of civilized enjoyment.

HAMSTERLEY AND JORROCKS

HAMSTERLEY AND JORROCKS

THE creator of Jorrocks, Robert Smith Surtees, always suppressed the fact that he was a novelist and was ready to quarrel with Harrison Ainsworth or any other editor who dared link his name with a magazine serial. So insistent was he in dissociating his squireship from his authorship that he deprived himself of notoriety in life and biographical fame in death. If we glance at the British Museum Catalogue we find four sparsely filled pages given to Surtees while one hundred and twenty crowded pages are devoted to Dickens. One writer, however, abhorred publicity and the other courted it. No society, as in the case of Dickens, could be organized to visit the localities described by Surtees or the houses in which he lived, for no one has definitely identified the "country" over which Jorrocks hunted. Some talk of Essex, some of Kent, and others of Surrey, Sussex, Yorkshire and Durham, yet the only place that can with certainty be associated with Surtees as a man is Hamsterley Hall, the house he inherited from his father.

It was to Hamsterley, therefore, on the Durham-Northumberland border, that I went to get not so much an impression of the author as of his setting. The place was said to be ancient and haunted and expecting to see a hoary stone manor I was surprised to be set down in front of a rectangular façade of

Strawberry Hill date. The back of the house, as I was to find out later, betrayed its mediæval origin, but to begin with I got a beaming impression of eighteenth-century enlightenment.

I think it must be Hamsterley Surtees had in mind when in *Hillingdon Hall* he describes the mansion as being of the "patchworky order partly stone, partly stucco . . . an old-fashioned manor house with panelled rooms on either side of the entrance," and "a new front containing a handsome drawing room, dining room and library." Gothic buildings of the Walpole date have a charm which they lost completely in the dawn of the nineteenth century, when on a basis of correct knowledge uninfused by fancy architects began to design fortress or minster-like abodes of varying sizes and the countryside and suburbs became studded with Ravensworths and Abbotsfords. There is nothing of the fortress or minster about the new front at Hamsterley and the machicolated finish to the top storey merely serves to emphasize the unaggressive outline of the building. Within, the light large Georgian rooms are far from conventual or baronial, though the windows by means of ogival woodwork are made to do obeisance to the general gothic fancy. Ceilings, decorations, and bookcases are neither heavy nor mediæval, for the same spirit that haunts chinoiserie lurks in this type of room.

I was told that the rebuilding had been done not by a Surtees but by a former owner, Henry Swinburne, who had inherited Hamsterley from an elder brother. My curiosity being aroused by the evidences of his taste I begged to be told something about him. He

was, they said, a Catholic gentleman raised in the
county who had got his first schooling at Scorton near
Catterick and his later education at the Lacelle Monastery in Paris. His tastes became those of a French-
man and residence at Bordeaux and Turin finally
endowed him with a glossy un-English polish. When
the moment came for him to take up his duties as squire
of Hamsterley he found himself ill-equipped for life in
the depths of the country, but nevertheless decided to
live on his property for part of the year. To help him
bear his fate he married a girl from a convent at Aix-
la-Chapelle and took her back to share the rustic
dullness of Durham.

Finding Hamsterley too gloomy for his pleasure and
too small for his requirements, he began to reconstruct
it, and one can read the date 1769 on some of the lead-
work. Rebuilding amused him for a while, but when
the novelty of introducing civilized fashions to the rude
county in which fate forced him to live had worn off,
nothing, not even the elegant transformation he had
wrought in a dumpy stone manor, could reconcile him
or his wife to hobnobbing with country neighbours or
to dark evenings at home. Presently they flitted away
to mingle in the more congenial life of the Continent.
We hear of Mrs. Swinburne receiving the Order of the
Croix Etoilée at the hands of Maria Theresa, of her
eldest son becoming page to Marie Antoinette, of a
journey to newly-ceded Trinidad where her husband
had been appointed *vendu* master, of Henry Swinburne's death there from sunstroke, of the monument
raised to his memory at San Juan. One day in 1803

the news filtered through to Hamsterley that its owner was dead. No child of his wished to live there and after a while the place was offered for sale. It was purchased by Robert Surtees of Milkwell Burn for his son, Anthony Surtees, who brought to Hamsterley Hall a small son, Robert Smith, aged four, whose home it became for fifty-seven years.

Robert Smith in company with little contemporary Blacketts and Loraines was sent to classes at Ovingham-on-Tyne, seven miles from Hamsterley, and later attended the famous Grammar School in Durham. Being a second son and without expectations he was then articled to Mr. Robert Purvis, a Newcastle solicitor, to get a grounding in law before proceeding to London to earn his living. In 1825 he went south for the first time by the express coach, Highflyer, which starting from Newcastle made the metropolis in thirty-six hours. This was considered "fine travelling." The fare for an inside seat was at this time six pounds, a peak pre-railway price, for thirteen years later we find "Boz" and "Phiz" able to buy two inside seats for Greta Bridge for the same sum.

From 1825 to 1828 Surtees lived in London at 27 Lincoln's Inn Fields and worked with Mr. William Bell of Bow Church Yard. In 1828 he bought a partnership in a solicitor's firm and began to practise. This venture turned out so badly that after recovering his purchase-money he abandoned the law and took seriously to writing. Leading even in London a more or less countrified life he made a habit in his leisure of hunting with packs of hounds on the outskirts of the city where he mixed with Cockney sportsmen and noted down their singularities. The London described by him in *Jaunts and Jollities* is still a small London surrounded by copses, pasture and stubbles wherein remnants of game are precariously preserved for the benefit of the commercial "gent." When Mr. Jorrocks of the *Jaunts* goes out shooting, he drives from his house in Great Coram Street to Brixton Hill and thence to Streatham Common where resides Mr. "Nosey" Browne, who, for a consideration, permits Cockney gunmen to tramp over his land.

Browne's place is small, a mere fifty acres, and he knows every live thing on it. There is "old Bess" the shabby hen pheasant that has managed to keep alive for two seasons, there are three partridges with nicknames, all that survive of a covey, and then there is "old Tom" the grey-backed hare who has run the gauntlet many a time. "Will Mr. Jorrocks," enquires "Nosey," "like to go hover the ten hacre field, or Thompson's stubbles or Tim's turnips?" Sportsmen, he is warned, are not allowed to follow up their quarry on the neighbouring land of Squire Cheatum, but Jorrocks, determined not to have a blank day, ambushes "old Tom" from a shed on the Browne estate and kills him. As he does so a hand grasps his shoulder and it is pointed out to him that since the toe of his boot is over the boundary he is poaching. Fined a guinea for trespass he gives notice of appeal. When the case comes on at Croydon Sessions Squire Cheatum is represented by voluble Serjeant Bumptious, who pleads that for such an offence as slaughtering Miss Cheatum's pet hare, the culprit should be sent to the treadmill for six months. In spite of the Serjeant's eloquence, the plea fails and the sentence is not revised though the conviction is upheld.

Surtees projects his own shadow across the *Jaunts* as "the Yorkshireman" who companions Jorrocks on some of his expeditions. One of his first successes was *Mr. Jorrocks Day with the Surrey Stag-hounds*. In this sketch he made play with a cunning doe nicknamed "old Tonbridge" that was regularly chased by the Surrey Hunt. Usually to be depended on to make a bee-line for home as soon as she was turned out of her cart, on the day written up by Surtees she did not carry out her accustomed run, but jumped into a passing "po-chay." When the post-chaise drew up at its destination, a public-house, the doe was seen by loafers to be gazing out of the window. With a guffaw she was at once driven back to go through her usual performance.

Surtees's stories of Cockney sport in Cockney land being recognized by contemporaries as real experiences were found by so much the more amusing. The very fact that fun should be made of sport by a sportsman was in a way a novelty, for, as Surtees himself said, no one at that time had written "anything in the sporting line that he was not prepared to swear to." The accepted convention was that journalists should treat sport punctiliously as a sacrosanct pastime on which the aristocracy spent their leisure. Surtees dared show that well-bred sportsmen and even dukes could be ridiculous, and that the hatters, butchers, and cheese-mongers, who were copying the gentry by going out with the Surrey packs, were getting quite a lot of vulgar though none the less hearty enjoyment out of so doing. His contention was that hunting, though at one time considered incompatible with sober tradesmanlike occupations, had begun "to reverberate through the whole of our social system."

Surtees was twenty-eight when he published over his own name *The Horseman's Manual*. This was the first and last time he broke with anonymity. The book brought him to the notice of Mr. Shury, editor of *The Sporting Magazine*. Mr. Shury complimented him on his work and made a note of his name in case he should ever want to make use of his services. His star contributor had for some years been Major C. J. Apperley, known to all sportsmen as Nimrod, and Nimrod was a very grand gentleman who took a serious view of hunting and hunting journalism. Treated in a princely way by the owners of *The Sporting Magazine*, he was provided with six horses and a salary of £1,500 a year, and on his tours of the Hunts exacted homage from Masters everywhere. When he visited Robert Smith's father, Anthony Surtees, at Hamsterley, he was met at the coach halt by a good horse on which to hack over to the Hall while the family carriage lumbered after piled with hunting kit, saddles and other impedimenta. Squire Anthony Surtees had welcomed him as "a guest from heaven," broached for him his best claret and had sat gossiping over the fire with him for a whole happy evening. The northern pastures like the southern wolds were hotbeds of spicy stories, but Major Apperley was not always amused by them. He affected a

shudder at hearing Lord Londonderry called "a vulpi-
cide" and at learning that Lady Londonderry, a Vane-
Tempest by birth, could not so much as "bear the cry
of dogs." What were the aristocracy coming to?

Next morning at a meet of Sir Matthew White Rid-
ley's hounds Apperley was presented by Robert Smith
to Mr. Marley, the Newcastle tailor, as "a gentleman
from London who had never been out hunting before
and wished to be instructed in the sport." Mr. Marley
at once offered to give the novice a lead across country
and they hunted together throughout the day. Even
the experienced "Nimrod" evinced astonishment at the
range of Marley's knowledge. It had all been poured
out [at the covert side and it was the opinion of
contemporary sportsmen that Robert Smith got his
first notion for Jorrocks from Mr. Marley and his
Pomponius Ego from Major Apperley.

Some hunting men though maintaining a deferential
attitude to Nimrod were disposed to resent his conceit. So swollen-headed did he become in the long run
that he was rash enough to quarrel with Mr. Shury.
Believing that the editor he despised for his ignorance
of sport could not possibly run *The Sporting Magazine*
without him, he flung an insult at him and bounced
off to Paris. His disappearance was Surtees's opportunity to get tried out as a sporting journalist. Egged
on by his friend Frank Sitwell of Barmoor Castle,
"Nim North" of *The Sporting Magazine* who told him
that between them they could cover all the hunts in
England, he applied at once to be taken on the staff as
"Nim South." Shury was pleased to give Surtees a

trial and in February (1830) published a short article by him entitled *Breaking Ground*. Three months later the signature "Nim South" was appended to *A Day with the Brighton Harriers*. When this "Day" had been read and approved by sportsmen further "Days" were commissioned and *Nim South's Southern Tour* became a feature of the magazine, a tour which included the East Sussex, Old Berkeley, V.W.H. and other packs. In November "Nim South" visited Leicestershire and wrote on the Quorn Kennels. At this time he was paying his own expenses, and it seems felt himself inadequately rewarded for contributions that were widely read and popular in clubs and country houses. With practice came facility and with success the conviction that he was "first fiddle in the hunting field in journalism." Presently Surtees, like Apperley before him, showed a disposition to ride roughshod over Shury. How irritating it was to have to discuss articles with an editor who was entirely inexperienced in sport of any kind, a mere "getter up of a magazine," and how different it would be if proprietor, editor and contributors were all real sportsmen, or failing this if a sportsman could contrive to purchase a controlling interest in the periodical! Insinuations of this kind evoked no response in Shury. He refused to be jockeyed from control and scoffed at the idea of covering Surtees's hunting expenses on the scale Apperley had exacted.

Failing to get his own way, "Nim South" abandoned *The Sporting Magazine* to float a rival periodical. Rudolph Ackerman, publisher of sporting prints, stood in with him, put up the money and assisted to plan *The*

New Sporting Magazine. Surtees carried with him
some of the contributors and advertisers from the old
magazine, but the greatest asset he provided was the
figure of Jorrocks, who made his debut in the third
number and immediately became an important factor in
the success of the new venture.

Hardly had Surtees settled himself into his editorial
chair than Apperley applied to become a contributor.
Owing to an entangling contract, presumably with
Shury, he intimated that his contributions must be sent
in on the quiet and printed anonymously. Surtees
closed at once with this offer and led off in his opening
number with an article by Apperley entitled *Characters of Hunting Countries.* To Surtees in early life
Nimrod had been an idol, and in one of his *Jaunts* he
describes a scene at Calais into which we may read
something of his hero-worship. Jorrocks is watching an Englishman on the station, "a middle-aged,
middle-statured man, dressed in a single-breasted green
riding coat, striped waistcoat, and drab trousers," the
very clothes in which he was painted by Maclise, in the
debonair portrait once in the possession of Sir John
Murray. With ears cocked he hears the fellow ask
whether there are any letters waiting for M. Apperley
or Nimrod. Nearly off his head with excitement,
Jorrocks drops plump on his knees shouting "Nimrod!" Then and there he begged "the first man of the
age" to dine with him. When the dinner came off in
Great Coram Street the health of "the most distinguished sportsman of the day" was proposed, and in
replying to the toast Apperley disclaimed the title and

in words that are among the most hackneyed of all the quotations from Surtees's much-quoted novels went on to say, "I have portrayed our great national sports in their brightest and most glowing colours . . . on sporting subjects my pen shall yield to none. Sport prevents effeminacy. What says Juvenal? What says Xenophon? Cicero? Horace? Virgil? What about the value they attached to *mens sana in corpore sano?*" He ended his speech by drinking to "the brightest and best of civic sportsmen, the great John Jorrocks."

There are moments when Surtees reminds one of Dickens. The *Jaunts* to Margate and Herne Bay, for example, challenge comparison with two of the *Sketches by Boz, The Tuggses at Ramsgate* and *The Steam Excursion,* but it is a comparison that only serves to indicate a deep divide. Surtees, who is photographic in method and objective in outlook, renders the manners and the clichés of the day accurately, whereas Dickens with his strong subjective bias interprets what he sees in the terms of his own emotions. In his early work Surtees delights in plain observation and takes notice of things Dickens would never have heeded. For example, in writing of a drive to London-sur-Mary (Brighton) on the box-seat of "The Age," the famous coach driven by amateurs, his eyes fell on the inert figure of King William being drawn along the sea front. Seeing that the King's nose is blue, he makes the sighing comment, "A sign that he too is mortal, for he feels the cold!"

As Jorrocks develops a complete personality he writes letters to contributors to *The New Sporting Maga-*

zine and, like the ventriloquist's doll, rates his creator whom he alleges to be jealous of him and totally ignorant of sport.

The early Jorrocks is more whimsical in some respects than the mature figure in *Handley Cross* and *Hillingdon Hall*. In the trips he makes by paddle-boat from London Bridge to the seaside he gives one the same sense of actuality that shines through the *Jaunt to Paris*. There is always a precision of description one does not get in Dickens, and whether it is the Channel crossing on the Royal George or the six-horse diligence at Calais with its single postilion on the stern-wheeler and its horses' heads adorned with nets, bells, and foxtails, or Jorrocks wrestling with the French of Madame de Genlis's phrase-book to explain his wants to the natives, one knows that it is a personal experience that is being recorded. Likewise when the running of Lord Seymour's horses or the arrival of the Citizen King Louis Philippe for the Sunday races on the Champs de Mars is written of, we have the conviction that the picture is as authentic as an accurate observer can make it.

In early days Surtees spent part of his vacations in France visiting those English sportsmen, who either for Beau Brummell's reason or for some delinquency lived at Calais and Boulogne. Though exiled they organized an imitation of the life they loved, set up a small race-course, chased foxes on the links by the sea, and hunted hares at Hardelot. Surtees and a friend are said to have hunted Cresswell's dwarf foxhounds for a short time and occasionally had a day with the

Samer Hounds, a kind of *châsse* in which the pack bolted the quarry and let the sportsmen kill the foxes. This hunt was a business concern providing gloves for postilions and brushes for their horses' heads. The accuracy of Surtees has, I think, been under-rated, for it is no exaggeration to say that the social world, its interests and idiosyncrasies, can be reconstructed from the pages of his novels as they can from those of no other contemporary. Surtees is a chronicler rather than an imaginative writer and his books are very long and meticulously detailed. If for example one wants to know how railways affected the habits of town and country, how ordinary people reacted to the Corn Laws, the Reform Bill, the Poor Laws or the Great Exhibition, one finds the answer in one or other of the novels. Travel in coaches and railways is carefully described. Women's fashions, men's fashions, ringlets going out and bagged hair coming in is noted. The effect on women's clothes of the ability to carry about by train "immense quantities of luggage," the advent of the hansom, the arrival of the book-stall, the 2*d*. post, the 1*d*. post—everything is there even to the way the introduction of the electric telegraph with its weather reports affected hunting, to say nothing of the incidence of the Drainage Act that "advanced agriculture more than all previous inventions and legislation put together."

We get to know what were the fashionable dogs, the pug, the yapping Skye, and Abelard the poodle. We also are shown life in country houses and castles, the exact furnishing, the paper on the walls, the woollen bell-pulls, the chair cushions, the antimacassars, the japanned work-tables, the hip-bath, the foot-bath, the four-poster. We attend the *thé dansant*, and partake of the buffet food, we watch the ladies in their flounced frocks and later in their crinolines. Lord Baldwin is right in saying that from the pages of Surtees the early and mid-Victorian eras may be re-created in all their multifarious social detail.

Surtees was in advance of the average opinions of his day. He was in favour of opening Museums and the National Gallery on Sundays, and of Sunday bands in parks. He advocated the cultivation of sugar beet and flax, allowed his tenants to course hares and destroy rabbits and set his face against the increase of game-preserving and battues which to him were foreign innovations and contrary to the English spirit in sport.

On behalf of *The New Sporting Magazine* he had to attend race-meetings, but his interest in flat-racing was slight, and as for steeplechasing he abhorred it. The sight of a good get-away from the covertside was worth all the races in the world to him, and as for steeple-chasing, he used to say it was neither hunting nor racing, but a hybrid sport doing great damage to land and fences.

*   *   *   *   *

Just as Surtees was making a great success of *The New Sporting Magazine* his journalistic career was cut short by the unexpected death of his elder brother on an Italian ship in the Mediterranean. As squire-elect of Hamsterley he felt it to be his duty to live in Durham, take up county work and assist his father in the management of estate and hounds. This decision obliged him to put *The New Sporting Magazine* up for sale and to insert into the December number for 1836 his editorial farewell.

Death now mowed down his family with unpleasant speed. His mother died in 1837 and his father the following year. He stood as a Tory for Gateshead in 1837: the election scenes described in *Hillingdon Hall*, when Jorrocks achieves his final apotheosis, have their origin in this experience. Though Surtees himself was defeated, Jorrocks wins the election by two votes, those of Quakers who had believed him to be a teetotaller, and in his speech after the poll declared himself in the words of "Conin'sby" one of the "Tory men with Vig measures."

By the end of 1838 Surtees was owner of Hamsterley and Master of Hounds; in 1841 he married, in 1842 became a J.P. and Deputy Lieutenant of the County. During the years that these transmutations were in progress he gathered his *Jaunts* into a volume for publication under the title *Jaunts and Jollities*. The book had a foreword by Major Apperley and plates by a young artist who called himself "Phiz" as a set-off to his employer's pen-name "Boz," most of whose *Pickwick* he had illustrated.

The mention of "Phiz" introduces the problem of the illustrated novel. How did it come about that twenty years after the Waverley romances had sold themselves in their thousands without illustrations, by the time Queen Victoria came to the throne no novel could be counted on to sell unless accompanied by plates? Perhaps the change originated in a get-rich-quick movement on the part of publishers, for imagine how tempting it must have been to issue a book in twelve to twenty monthly parts at a shilling each with the certainty of selling it in volume form for a guinea and a half later on! Or could it have been due to the new fashion in humour that set in under William IV and resulted in such a blossoming of comic annuals, comic sketch-books and comic tales? It was the age of Hook, Barham and Hood, pantomime and comedietta that produced Jorrocks and Pickwick and what may be called the friendly, family spirit in literature, the spirit that is perpetuated in *Punch*. Mirth and joviality being the key-notes of the time, what more natural than that scenes of eating, drinking, sport and high-jinks generally should in the phraseology of the day be "improved" by illustrations? What mattered it that the same artist might be called on to design plates for *The Ingoldsby Legends, Demonology and Witchcraft*, the *Memoirs of Grimaldi*, to say nothing of the works of Harrison Ainsworth, Dickens and Mrs. Ewing? George Cruikshank, rather unfortunately for readers, worked for seventy years designing plates for books, and I sometimes think that he and the almost equally prolific Phiz may be responsible for giving one the impression that the Dickens novels are a continuum like a film sequence. The public gulped at the pictured serial, and the quick turnover encouraged novelists to publish while their books were being written, which accounts for the looseness and plotlessness of many of the novels of the day. The presses were always thundering in the writers' ears, a condition that Scott once said he found it stimulating to work under. Young authors living in the dawn of the serial boom soon realized the advantage of becoming editors themselves, and we find Ainsworth, Dickens and Surtees all taking charge of magazines into which they could insert as much or as little of their own work as they pleased and could choose their own artists.

The great importance attached to illustrations is clearly evidenced in the publication of *Handley Cross*, which was originally issued without plates, Henry Colburn having decided that the novel was in such bad taste that he could not spend money on its production. And the result was that the first edition did not sell. *Pickwick*, on the other hand, was in the beginning a narrative spun round illustrations. Commissioned by Chapman and Hall to link together the "Cockney Sporting Plates" of Robert Seymour (an artist in the pay of the firm who had already on their behalf illustrated Ovid, Wordsworth, Shakespeare and Southey at half a guinea a plate), the very young author of *Sketches by Boz* was told that his text must be little more than "a running accompaniment—like an ornamental border round the drawings." He was in fact to do something in the fashionably squibbish manner of some unsigned *Jaunts* that had been appearing in the pages of *The New Sporting Magazine*. He must concoct a kind of "Nimrod" club whose members shot and fished and got themselves into scrapes for want of experience. There was a huge public ready to enjoy fun of this kind and that public must be catered for.   Dickens, who felt no inclination whatever to model himself upon the *Jaunts* or act as "padder-out" to Seymour, protested that the idea was stale, but since he had his living to get and was engaged to be married he accepted the commission.

The "Nimrod" idea was soon jettisoned and in reading *Pickwick* one can see by the way he dallies over military gallantries at Rochester and social life at Dingley Dell how difficult the Cockney author found it to plunge his characters into country life.   He had been careful to tell his publisher the only kind of sport he knew anything about was "locomotion," in other words, the riding and posting he had been through as a press reporter, all of which had made him hate horses. When Winkle's mount "runs backwards" jerking Winkle from the saddle the author describes him as having "a tug of war" with the animal and being pulled along the ground by the bridle.   When Mr. Pickwick's four-wheel shay "smashes itself" against a wooden bridge, the horse has to be led to a stable seven miles away and Mr. Pickwick toys with the notion of "cutting the horse's throat!"   "It is like a dream," he sighs, "a hideous dream.   The idea of a man walking about all day with a dreadful horse he cannot get rid of!"   These equine adventures were matched by a day with the guns.   Mr. Pickwick is trundled through the fields and one of the party exclaims, as if to convince us that we really are in the country, "That's a fine piece of turf!"   Rather nervous at the way Winkle is handling his gun, Mr. Pickwick insists that he must carry it gunstock up.   Tupman is made to carry his in the same way and the pair of them are said to look like privates at a royal funeral, which reminds us that the only persons Dickens could have seen using firearms were the soldiers and sailors in a dockyard. He sends boys shinning up trees to shake young rooks from their nests for Winkle to pot at and watches partridges "strutting amongst the stubble unconscious of their approaching doom." There is a great lightening of humour when, shaking off the sporting club fetters, Dickens allows his own genius to take charge of the narrative.

Unlike the author of *Pickwick*, Surtees knew everything there was to know about sport and country life, but for all that no one of his novels ever rocketed into public favour. The *Jaunts and Jollities* sold quietly and *Handley Cross* took years to find its level. Surtees, though he could place his books, was never courted for contracts by several publishers at once. Indeed his experience was far from head-turning, and after the *Jaunts* had come out he felt the effect of the Dickens boom in the defection of "Phiz," who declaring himself "overwhelmed with orders" declined further work for Mr. Surtees. With "Phiz" "Boz" it seemed had struck up one of his close friendships. Together they had travelled to Greta Bridge to investigate "the cheap schools of the north" with a view to pillorying them in his new novel, *Nicholas Nickleby*. They had stayed at Barnard Castle in the early part of 1838, and though it would have been possible for "Phiz" to take "Boz" on to Hamsterley, there is nothing to show that he did so.

I found that memories of Dickens still linger in the

north. From the drawing-room window of the King's Head, Barnard Castle, the site of what had been Master Humphrey the clockmaker's shop, was pointed out to me by an old waiter who assured me that the idea for a series of stories to be covered by the title *Master Humphrey's Clock* had come to Dickens in that very room and that Mr. Dickens had gone across the main street to get Mr. Humphrey to tell him what he could about the local boarding schools.

I do not know whether Surtees and Dickens ever met except perhaps casually in the Law Courts, and in a way it seems odd that they should ever have come within comparing distance in print, for in spite of the Jorrocks-Pickwick concatenation, a purely involuntary affair, they are literally worlds apart. For tombstone information it should perhaps be stated that Robert Smith Surtees was born in 1803 and Charles Dickens in 1812. Surtees was the son of a country gentleman and Dickens the son of a paymaster in the Navy; one boy was learning to shoot and ride at ten and the other at the same age labelling blacking bottles. The childhood of one was spent among the woods and fields of Durham and that of the other in Seven Dials and Camden Town. In spite of the disparity in age both were teaching themselves to write in the Law Courts at the same time. It can be no mere accident that one recognizes the affinity of Serjeant Buzfuz of Dickens and Serjeant Bumptious of Surtees. Both characters must have been suggested by some original observed by both men, probably the well-known Serjeant Bompas, then a leader in the Court of Common Pleas. And we can

see how this might have come about, for Surtees quali-
fied as a solicitor in 1828 and prior to this lodged for
three years in Lincoln's Inn Fields haunting the Courts,
while Dickens, a shorthand writer in Doctors' Commons, spent much of his spare time also in the Courts.
Both young men were inveterate scribblers and both
out to make a living by their wits. Shortly before
Dickens gave up newspaper reporting for authorship
Surtees abandoned the law for journalism. Surtees
was always the countryman in London and an aristocrat
at heart, while Dickens was a democrat to his finger-tips.
Surtees had the "county" outlook on life and was inclined to regard the middle-class man not as a being in
himself but as a caricature of a gentleman, which tends
to give a burlesque flavour to much of his writing.
Being unimaginative and sharply observant, we never
catch him feeling with his characters or viewing them
as objects of compassion. They are always material for
humorous treatment. Surtees tilted his nose and spoke
of the people as "the great unwashed," whereas Dickens,
quite indifferent whether they washed or not, just loved
them. Surtees was acutely class-conscious, showed a
contemptuous Georgian point of view about "the sex";
Dickens, sentimental, warm-hearted, idealizer of women,
was devoid of class-consciousness. Surtees presents to
us the world of wealth and amusement what Jorrocks
dubbed "the rich man's paradise" and Dickens the
morass or "poor man's puggatory" in which the pillars
of that world had their foundation. The climber has
always provoked mirth but the resolution needed to
gratify snobbishness may partly account for the tough-

ness and strength of the ruling class in England, for authority in English life has always been replenished from below. Moreover, the existence of the upper classes, then as now, was considered so agreeable as to be a sufficient reward for all the struggling and contriving of tradesmen and financiers. Life in England has not changed in this respect, for the merchant and the Jew, now as always, have found their easiest approach to coveted social prizes in the organized hunts and have shown their essential grit by choosing to compete with the "county" on its own ground.

*   *   *   *   *

Surtees was in a strong position for satirizing his contemporaries. He had been brought up from childhood to follow hounds first with his father's pack and then with that most famous of Durham Masters, Mr. Lambton. He could not go wrong in any matter connected with horses and hounds, but though people of his own kind might appreciate his squibbish humour, there were some among them who thought he cheapened sport and faintly resented the fun he poked at hunting men and landlords and the vulgarity with which he invested them. The majority of his readers trusted him, for it was impossible that such an expert could mortally offend the susceptibilities of sportsmen. In his "Days" with packs of hounds he never attempted to imitate Nimrod, in flattering the Masters who had showed him sport, for he was an independent fellow with no particular wish to please and was more

210

concerned with the antics of the middle-class sportsmen who with the introduction of railway travelling were invading preserves hitherto sacred to the landed gentry and their dependants than with orthodox sportsmen. In a sense Surtees may be said to have originated the comic figure in sport. Addison's fox-hunter and Squire Western have their niches but neither of them is really comparable with Mr. Jorrocks.

Unlike Surtees, Dickens was no mere chronicler or spectator of events, for he infused all characters and all situations with his peculiar sense of pathos, humour and idealism. With the incandescent genial power that was his birthright he tilted against social injustice in every form and created a London, mysterious, gloomy, and gay, peopled by individuals of indestructible quality. To write the novels of Charles Dickens a man must appreciate that life is a serious undertaking, to write those of Surtees it is merely necessary to appreciate the importance of field sports in the England of that day.

*   *   *   *   *

As a Durham squire, Surtees continued to contribute to *The New Sporting Magazine*, and it was at Hamsterley that the most famous of the anonymous novels was composed during the years 1836–7. Later to be called *Handley Cross*, the story made its first appearance serially in *The New Sporting Magazine* as *The Gin and Water Hounds* (March 1838). *The Gin and Water Hounds* ran into twenty chapters and ended with the lunacy enquiry. When these chapters were reprinted as a three-volume novel further matter was added and Jorrocks's *Lectures on Hunting* were included in the book.

Handley Cross, as we have seen, was an anxiety to its publisher. Henry Colburn was always sensitive about upper-class opinion and anxious not to give offence. The character, doings and sayings of Jorrocks made him so apprehensive that he actually advised Surtees to cut the fellow out of the story. The author was immensely taken aback by Colburn's disapproval, for he had got it firmly fixed in his head that *Handley Cross* was the best thing he had ever done, a verdict posterity has endorsed.

The story of *Handley Cross* is too well known to too many people for me to do more than indicate its nature. Handley Cross is an inland spa eager to attract winter residents. John Jorrocks, a London grocer, whose fame has percolated to the provinces and whose wealth qualifies him for the position, is invited to become Master of the local farmers' hunt. He accepts the proposal with delight and transfers himself, wife and staff to Handley Cross, where he hunts the hounds for a season. His friends in London think him mad to waste large sums of money in this way and proceed to have him certified as a lunatic. At this point the first version of the novel ends. In the amplified version Jorrocks is delivered from Hoxton Asylum by the Lord Chancellor himself and is able to go on hunting with his huntsman, James Pigg, for as many seasons as he pleases.

In Colburn's eyes the novel had several doubtful features: it caricatured the original Jorrocks of the *Jaunts* and it caricatured Nimrod.   Instead of being the debonair deity depicted in the *Jaunt to Paris* he figures as Pomponius Ego, a swaggering, snobbish sportsman.   In a famous chapter Jorrocks invites Mr. Hego to visit his "most provincial pack" (the self-denigration is almost Chinese!) and the Master of the Handley Cross Hounds is depicted as "all of a tremble" as to what the great man will say.   When elegant Pomponius turns up at the meet and casts a patronizing eye over horses, hunt servants, and hounds, the Master quakes with apprehension, but after a good run an anxious morning is redeemed by a wonderful evening during which Pomponius with well-timed conde-scension gets off his high horse and exchanges hunting reminiscences with the gratified grocer.

Handley Cross, the most thumbed of all Surtees's books, still provokes lively discussion, for there are still people who like arguing about the locality in which the scenes are set.   Was it Leamington Spa or Ash-ford, or Shotley Bridge itself?   Some noting that Pigg sailed from the north in a collier to Deal and travelled on into the Vale of Sheepwash whence he could see the sea on the horizon, were sure it was Kent that Surtees describes.   But there are others who say that though Pigg was "Newcassel" born and bred, they know of a Sheepwash near Hamsterley and that not far from Sedgefield the sea is visible.   Some of Surtees's place-names do not exist in Kent, for example Winforth Rig, Howell Burn, Corsenside Lane, and there is a certain

Northumbrian twist in some of the descriptions and we may take it that when it is not Northumberland it is Surrey, and when it is not Kent it is Sussex, and when none of these places it may be Durham.   After all, his experiences as a sporting journalist were wide.   I like to think, however, that he took his notions of what life was like at an English spa not only from fashionable Harrogate but from the modest spa flourishing at his own gate.   Hamsterley is close to Shotley Bridge, which, like Croft, Gilsland, Dinsdale, and other northern spas, has now ceased to function.   I assured myself, however, that the spring from which the glasses of curative water were once dispensed still flows under the shelter of its gothic-roofed summer house.   The policies, where patients once sipped their medicinal draughts while sauntering up and down to music, are now used for girl-guide rallies or flower shows.   The notice-boards that stand around in various stages of decay make it hard to imagine that so neglected and forlorn a spot can ever have been a rendezvous of fashion.

* * * * *

Surtees had a great love of the country and it is doubtful whether Dickens, who disliked the country and was even bored during his honeymoon in Chalk village, had any feeling for nature other than human nature.   He had, however, a great sense of theatrical effects and used scenery and natural phenomena rather as a scene painter does to enhance the significance of his production.   A thunderstorm, a lurid sky, a streaming

214

day, lush meadows, singing birds, properties all, in the
sense in which they were used by Edgar Allen Poe.
The sea, the wind, the trees were but accompaniment
to the poet's thoughts, they had no value in themselves,
and so I think it must have been with Dickens.   In
spite of Surtees's cheap cynicism and superficiality he
had one deep quality, a love of nature for her own sake.
It was something quite different from any Words-
worthian glimpse of God: it was neither philosophical
nor poetic in the ordinary sense, but at any rate it was
sensitive and correct being the ingrained feeling of a
country gentleman with a long line of country gentlemen behind him.   Here is a description of a day at the
turn of the year; it may be February.   There is bright
sun and a white frost and no sign of spring.

> It was neither a day for fishing or hunting, nor coursing,
> nor anything but farming.   The country, save where there
> were a few lingering patches of turnips, was all one dingy
> drab, with abundant scalds on the undrained fallows.   The
> grass was more like hemp than anything else.   The very
> rushes were sickly and yellow.

Again of an autumn landscape he writes:

> It was a fine view.   Three parts of the hill are encircled
> with fertile pastures and productive cornfields, while the
> fourth stretches away, far as the eye can reach, in undulating
> and occasionally broken moorland ground.   The fertile
> patches irrigating the whole were dotted over with little
> black-faced sheep, while from the then browning heather
> the wild and scared muir-fowl rose in noisy clamour, winging
> their way to quieter regions in the distance.

And here is the setting for a steeplechase:

The great event was ushered in by one of those fine, bright autumnal days that shame many summer ones, and seem inclined to carry the winter months over into the coming year. The sun rose with effulgent radiance, gilding the lingering brown and yellow autumn tints and lighting up the landscape with searching inquisitorial scrutiny. Not a nook, not a dell, not a cot, not a curl of smoke but was visible, and the whole scene shone with the vigour of a newly burnished, newly varnished picture. The cattle stood in bold relief against the perennially green fields, and the newly dipped lambs dotted the hill-sides like white marbles. A clear bright light gleamed through the stems of the Scotch fir belt, encircling the brow of High Rays Hill, giving goodly promise of continued fineness.

These are water-colours in the best English manner and stand out in definite contrast to the less sensitive generalizations indulged in by Dickens. Of summer "Boz" writes:

There is no month in the whole year in which nature wears a more beautiful appearance than in the month of August. Spring has many beauties, and May is a fresh and blooming month, but the charms of this time of the year are enhanced by their contrast with the winter season. August has no such advantage. It comes when we remember nothing but clear skies, when the recollection of snow and ice has faded from our minds etc.

And again:

The June weather was delicious. The sky was blue, the larks soaring high over the green corn, I thought all that country-side more beautiful and peaceful by far than I had ever known it to be yet.

The most generally admired description of scenery by Dickens is that of the marsh in *Great Expectations*:

> It was a dark night though the full moon rose as I left the enclosed lands and passed out upon the marshes. Beyond their dark line there was a ribbon of clear sky, hardly broad enough to hold the red large moon. . . .

But this too is but the painted backcloth to the action of the story. Dickens has no occasion for landscape as an end in itself and his use of it is completely alien to the wide-eyed observation of the country-bred squire. He is so subjectively occupied that he feels "the shudder of the dying day in every blade of grass." I am glad to have been brought up in the deep silences of Northamptonshire woods and fields and to have been dependent on myself for amusement, for it gave one an ineradicable understanding of wind and trees and conditions of country life. In a sense, one can interpret nature and her moods and it enables one to admire the old-fashioned sportsman with his sensibility and his instinctive understanding, the qualities that are fast fading from general consciousness. Not only do broadcasted weather reports tend to destroy the countryman's sense of atmospheric change, but the old inherited wisdom is vanishing and we are as likely as not to be answered, if we ask of some shepherd, "Will it be fine tomorrow?" with the reply, "Last night's wireless said it would." We cannot, however, rob the animals of their birthright: ducks still know if the season is to be dry or wet and site their nests accordingly, rooks know when to begin twig-breaking and cattle whether it is to be rainy or fine.

Durham county has always been renowned for its sportsmen and one hears from the old so many stories about them that it is as if their ghosts still haunted the countryside. Sedgefield, at one time the Melton of the north, was once described as one of the three towns best worth living in, the other two being London and Paris! At Sedgefield one is not allowed to forget Mr. Lambton, the man who schooled Surtees in the hunting field, Mr. Lambton with his quiet sense of humour and his funny gentle manner. He preserved for posterity one of his strange talks with William IV, a monarch at no time remarkable for his quickness of wit. Dining at Windsor he found himself the butt of royal curiosity.

"Pray, Mr. Lambton," kindly enquired the King, "how old may you be?"

"Sixty-seven, may it please your Majesty," dutifully replied his guest.

"Mr. Lambton," continued the King, "pray who was your mother?"

" My mother, Sir, was a Lyon."

"A lion," enquired the monarch dubiously, "but how *can* that be?"

And it is not Mr. Lambton only that men remember as they go about the country. Many a hunting man as he motors the straight road from Middleton to Yarm calls to mind how Nimrod on that very road met the Stockton locomotive, the original "puffing billy," and again as he passes Newton House (now a hotel) on his way to Catterick he may give a moment's thought to Lord Darlington, whose "commodious hunting box" it was, and who there used to feed his own hounds with his own hands.

As we think of these old-fashioned sportsmen brought up in closest touch with nature we cannot help finding for them a soft spot in our hearts. They tried to play nature's game in nature's way, and somehow the life they led developed some sort of reliability and character, a different sort of character and perhaps more resourceful than that brought out by taking part in organized games in which opponents obey rules and can be penalized for infringing them. Surtees had no use for games of any kind, for unexpected things cannot very well happen in games, but with nature anything may happen, bells and whistles do not bring her to heel. With nature each man has to do his own reckoning: a horse may put him down, a fox may foul a line among sheep, a short rising trout may balk him. Surtees manages with clearness and sincerity to interpret the actual feeling of the man to whom such things happen, to give his sense of enjoyment and his disappointment, generations of men have got the same thrill out of reading his books as they do from a fast run or from playing a good fish. As Surtees himself said, "The sporting world is altogether different from the general world of literature, a book serving many sportsmen for a long time. Some indeed get on capitally without any."

* * * * *

Men who are not given to reading will adopt a Surtees novel as their only literature, and that is why Surtees's phrases used to be in every subaltern's mouth and why correspondents in *The Field* were once politely requested to use no "threadbare Jorrocks witticisms." And yet Surtees does not write always about hunting. William Morris, who admired Surtees immensely as "a master of life," placed him in the same rank as Dickens. Thackeray was envious of his power of characterization, and Kipling in *My Son's Wife* makes Frankwell Midmore, a townsman who inherits a country place, identify all the characters he met in his new life "out of the natural history books by Mr. Surtees . . . Dickens and horsedung characters," but true types. The writings of this Durham squire are really documentary and from their pages we may get to know the farmer, the land agent, the county solicitor, the squire, as well as the odd man and the butler in the houses of the great and from them reconstruct the interests and temper of the day. The warp and woof of existence in Victorian days is presented in great detail and no survey of English life at this period is complete without reference to the Surtees novels, which are strangely observant and brimming with vitality. There is no sign of art or effort in any of them: they just bubble along from day to day filled with commonplace happenings and commonplace people and in their entirety make an unchallengeable picture of English rural life.

No one of Surtees's other books has enjoyed the sustained popularity of *Handley Cross*, though *Mr.*

Sponge's Sporting Tour, written to decry the betting-list system, had a more immediate success owing probably to the Leech illustrations. *Young Tom's Heartaches and Horses,* in spite of its allusions to the Great Exhibition, proved difficult to market. It was offered to *Punch* and declined by Mark Lemon, who advised Surtees to remodel it as a diary. Harrison Ainsworth for old friendship's sake gave it a run in the *New Monthly Magazine,* but readers found it wearisome and the author was told to "wind up the tale as quickly as he could." When Surtees persisted in carrying on with it Ainsworth wrote sharply, "I have no wish the tale should be continued." *Ask Mamma* and *Plain or Ringlets* were frankly advertised as plotless, continuous narratives. They achieved a fair circulation owing to Leech, but in general were pronounced by contemporaries to be monotonous.

During the winter evenings and in summer-time at Hamsterley, Surtees had plenty of time on his hands. Like Victor Hugo he stood at a tall desk to write and his pen travelled rapidly over the thin blue quarto sheets of paper before him. All his novels were composed at Hamsterley, and though every crevice of the house has been searched for his manuscripts, nothing has been found but a few pages of *Mr. Facey Romford's Hounds* which have been clenched in some hand as if for the waste-paper basket. The sheets that have escaped destruction show that his handwriting was cursive, rapidly executed and heavily corrected. It may be that even these fragments owe their preservation to the fact that *Mr. Facey* was a posthumously published book. Having maintained a strict anonymity throughout life, Surtees probably meant to leave no trace of his literary activities behind, but he happened to die while on a visit to Brighton, and possibly for this reason a few pages of manuscript were left undestroyed.

Surtees always used to say in his lifetime that though Durham was a glorious country to hunt in, it must soon be ruined. Not that there was any menace from collieries in his corner of the county, but like all sportsmen of his generation, he viewed the railway break-through with apprehension and like Mr. Weller regarded the locomotive as "unconstitootional and an inwader of privileges." Fighting to the last against the inevitable, he managed to deflect a line it was proposed to build from Consett to Newcastle and rather fortunately for him did not live to see constructed the viaduct over the Pont Valley close to Hamsterley. The contract indeed was only signed after his death. He lived long enough, however, to suffer great unhappiness in watching a track being cut through the preserves of the Hurworth Hunt that he feared would threaten the amenities of Mr. Lambton's kennels at Sedgefield.

Towards the close of his life Surtees lost his nerve and might be observed on hunting days riding a white pony and making use of his intimate knowledge of the countryside to get quickly from point to point. He was by then sure that hunting would soon become "a mere matter of history," but at any rate till the war began in 1939 hounds met and foxes showed sport in the very country over which he had ridden a century before. Moreover, since it is said that more people were hunting in England in 1930 than ever hunted before, his earlier statement that "hunting was bound to reverberate through the whole of our social system," proved the better forecast. Though unsuspected by Surtees the real enemy of the sport in England was not the railway he feared, but the war taxation of which he had never heard and the sorry victor in the contest no mechanized monster, but the Chancellor of the Exchequer himself.

Printed in Great Britain by
Butler & Tanner Ltd.,
Frome and London